wire mothers

Other books about scientists from G.T. Labs

SAFECRACKER: A TWO-FISTED SCIENCE COMIC

TWO-FISTED SCIENCE: STORIES ABOUT SCIENTISTS

WILD PERSON IN THE WOODS

DIGNIFYING SCIENCE: STORIES ABOUT WOMEN SCIENTISTS

"TALKING" ORANGUTANS IN BORNEO (FOR THE ORANGUTAN FOUNDATION INTERNATIONAL)

FALLOUT: J. ROBERT OPPENHEIMER, LEO SZILARD, AND THE POLITICAL SCIENCE OF THE ATOMIC BOMB

SUSPENDED IN LANGUAGE: NIELS BOHR'S LIFE, DISCOVERIES, AND THE CENTURY HE SHAPED

BONE SHARPS, COWBOYS, AND THUNDER LIZARDS: EDWARD DRINKER COPE, OTHNIEL CHARLES MARSH, AND THE GILDED AGE OF PALEONTOLOGY

LEVITATION: PHYSICS AND PSYCHOLOGY IN THE SERVICE OF DECEPTION

ALSO

CHARLES R. KNIGHT: AUTOBIOGRAPHY OF AN ARTIST

wire mothers:
harry harlow and
the science of love

jim ottaviani / dylan meconis

G.T. LABS

WIRE MOTHERS
HARRY HARLOW AND THE SCIENCE OF LOVE

First Edition: July, 2007

ISBN 978-0-9788037-1-1
ISBN 978-0-9660106-9-5 (set)

Library of Congress Control Number: 2007900136

Part of a series of books on the science of the unscientific, which also includes *Levitation: Physics and Psychology in the Service of Deception.*

A General Tektronics Labs book.

G.T. Labs
P.O. Box 8145
Ann Arbor, MI 48107

info@gt-labs.com
www.gt-labs.com

5 4 3 2 1

We tend to love as did our mother
Cloth or wire or any other...

-- H. Harlow

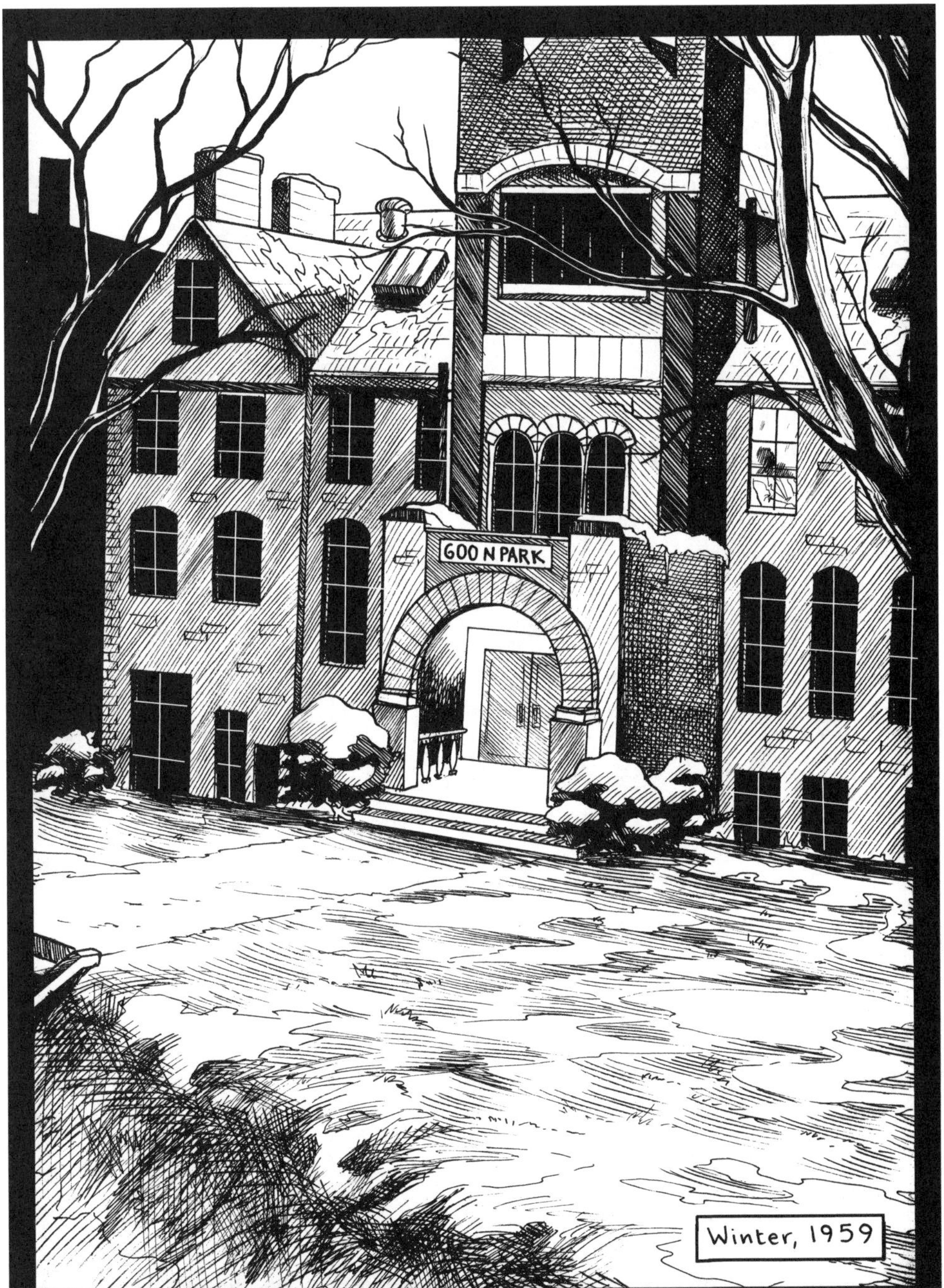
600 N PARK
Winter, 1959

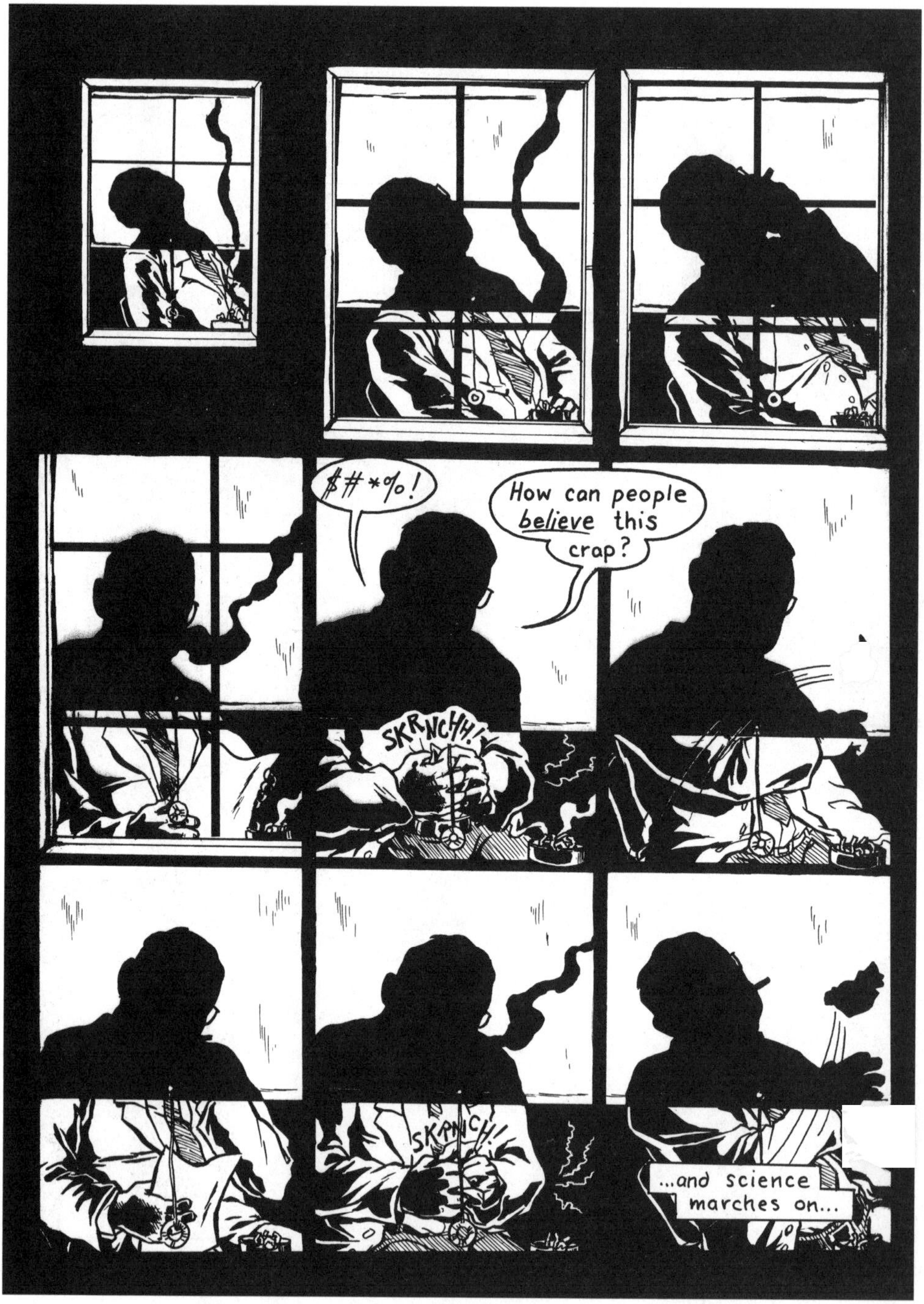
$#*%!
How can people believe this crap?
SKRNCHH!
SKRNCH!
...and science marches on...

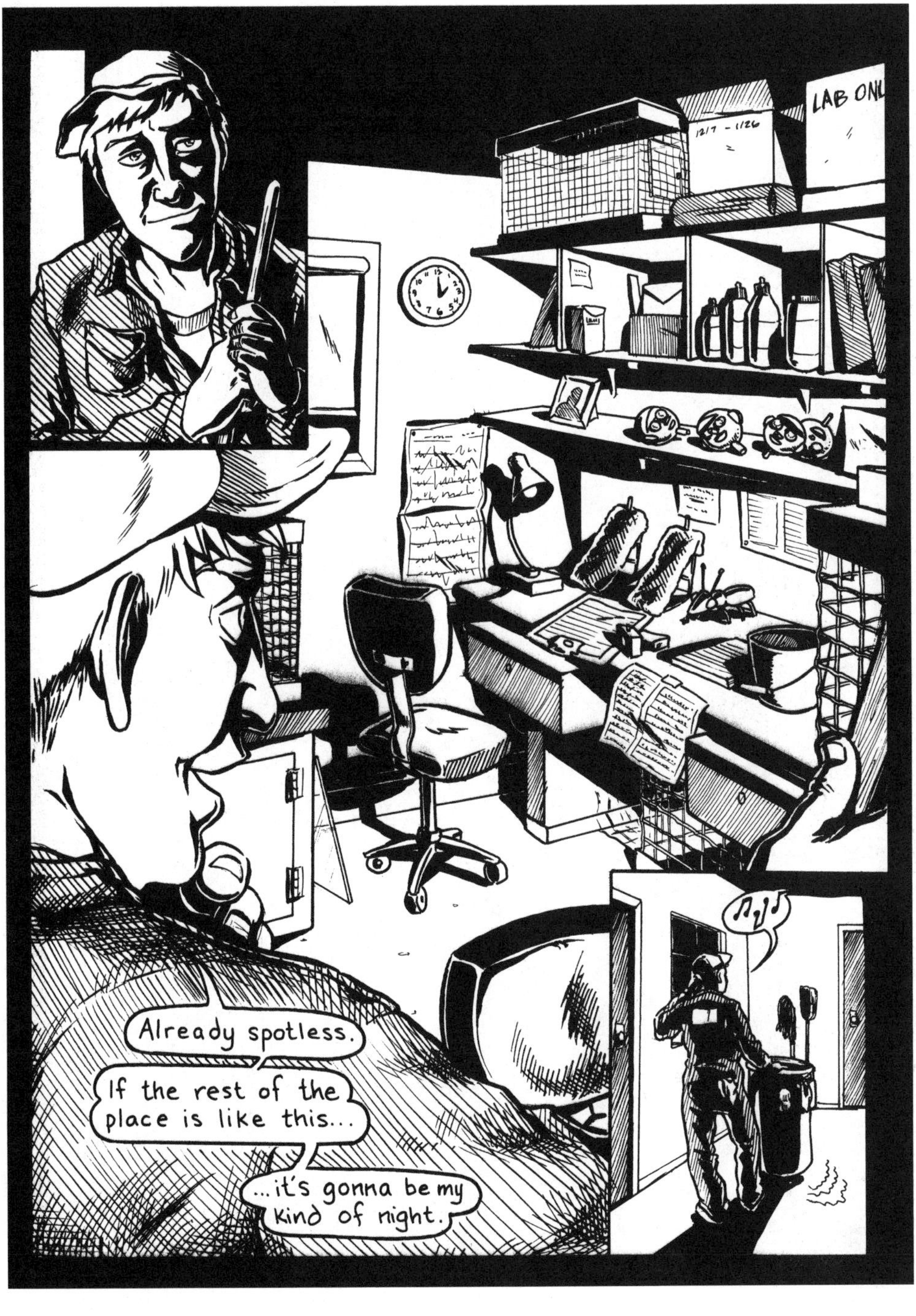
LAB ONL
12/7 - 1/26
Already spotless.
If the rest of the place is like this...
...it's gonna be my kind of night.

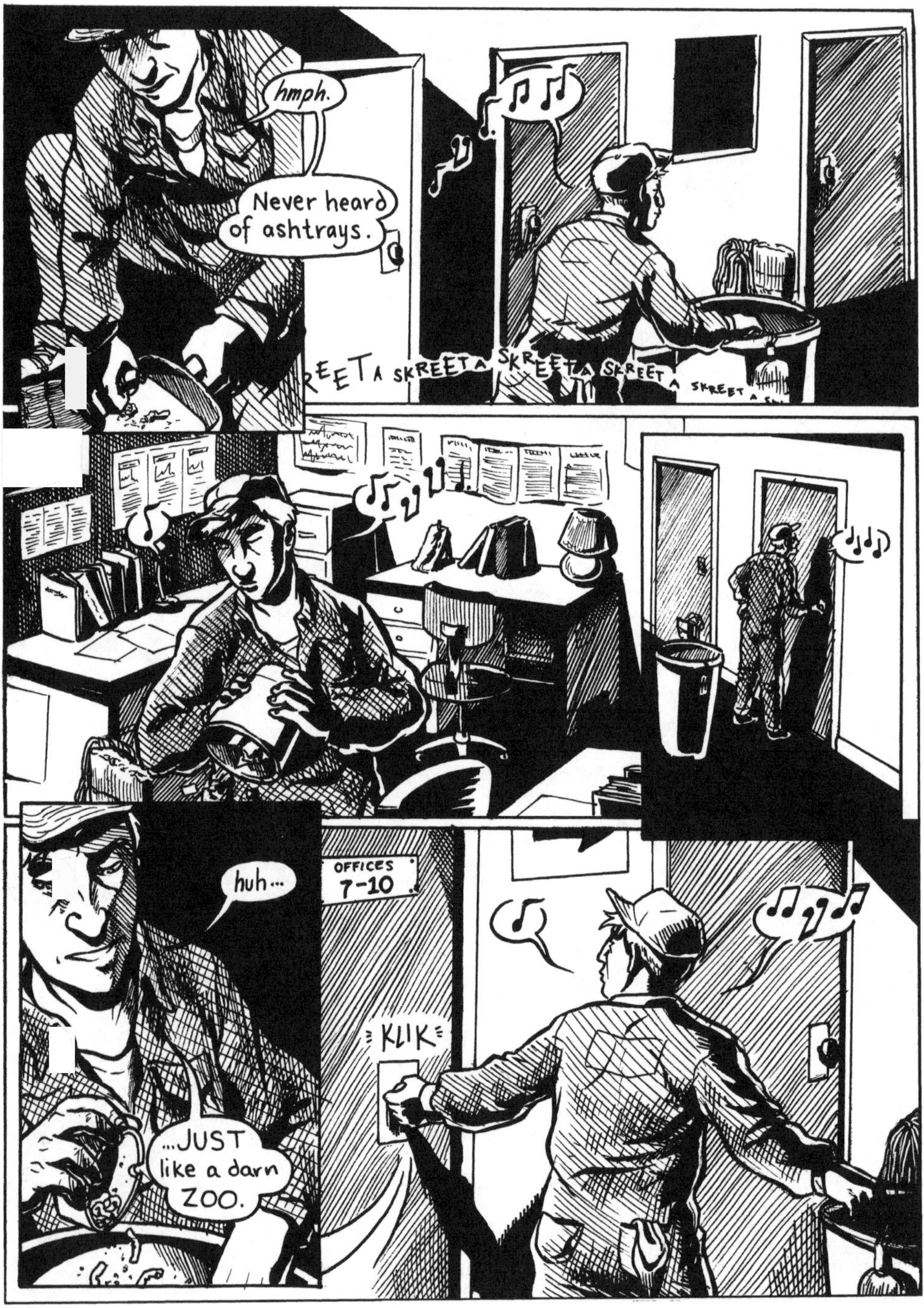
hmph.
Never heard of ashtrays.
SKREET A SKREET A SKREET A SKREET A SKREET A SKREET A
huh...
...JUST like a darn ZOO.
OFFICES 7-10
KLIK

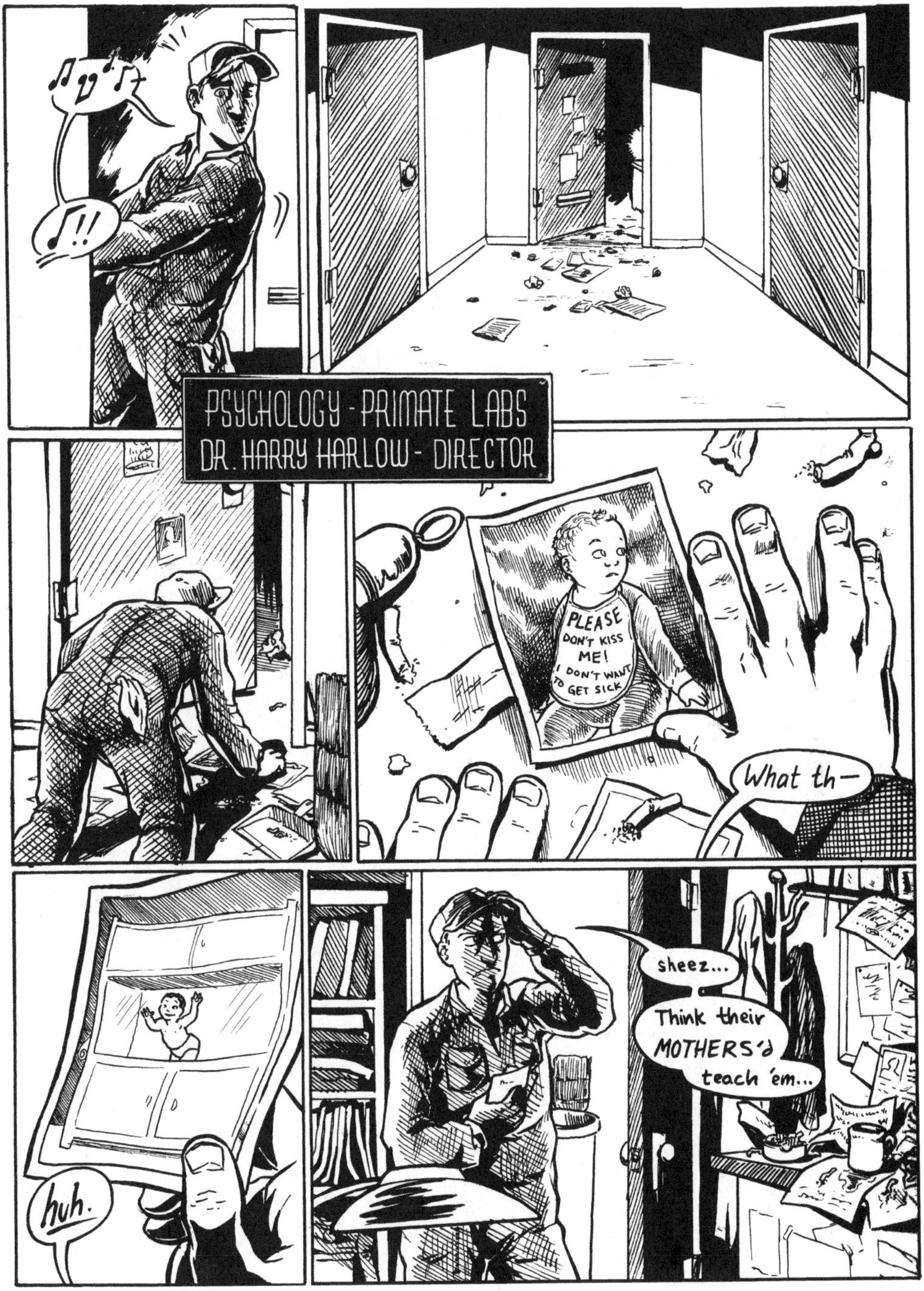
♫!!
PSYCHOLOGY - PRIMATE LABS
DR. HARRY HARLOW - DIRECTOR
PLEASE DON'T KISS ME! I DON'T WANT TO GET SICK
What th—
huh.
sheez...
Think their MOTHERS'd teach 'em...

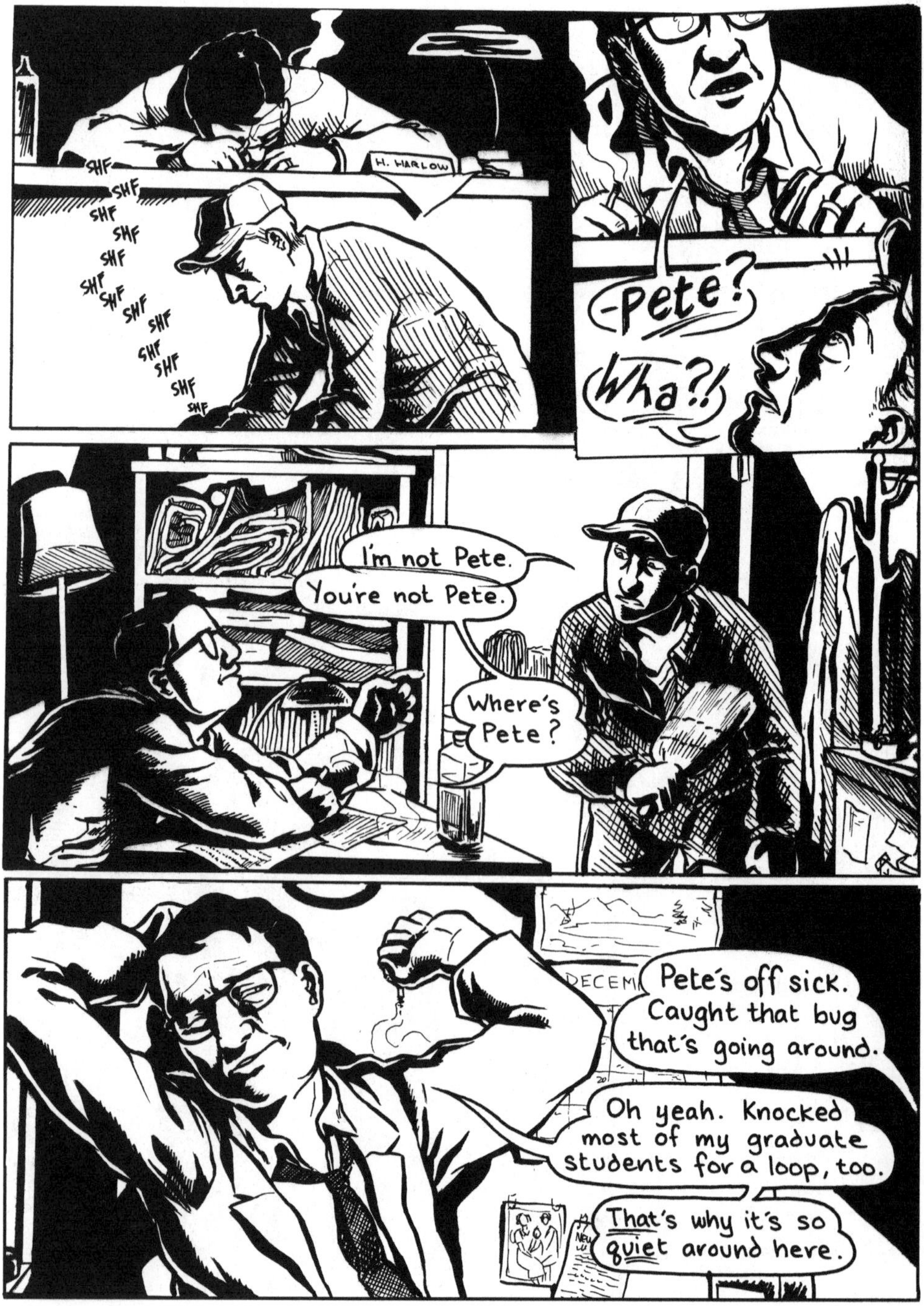
H. WARLOW
SHF
SHF
SHF
SHF
SHF
SHF
SHF
SHF
SHF
SHF
SHF
SHF
SHF
-Pete?
Wha?!
I'm not Pete.
You're not Pete.
Where's Pete?
Pete's off sick. Caught that bug that's going around.
Oh yeah. Knocked most of my graduate students for a loop, too.
That's why it's so quiet around here.

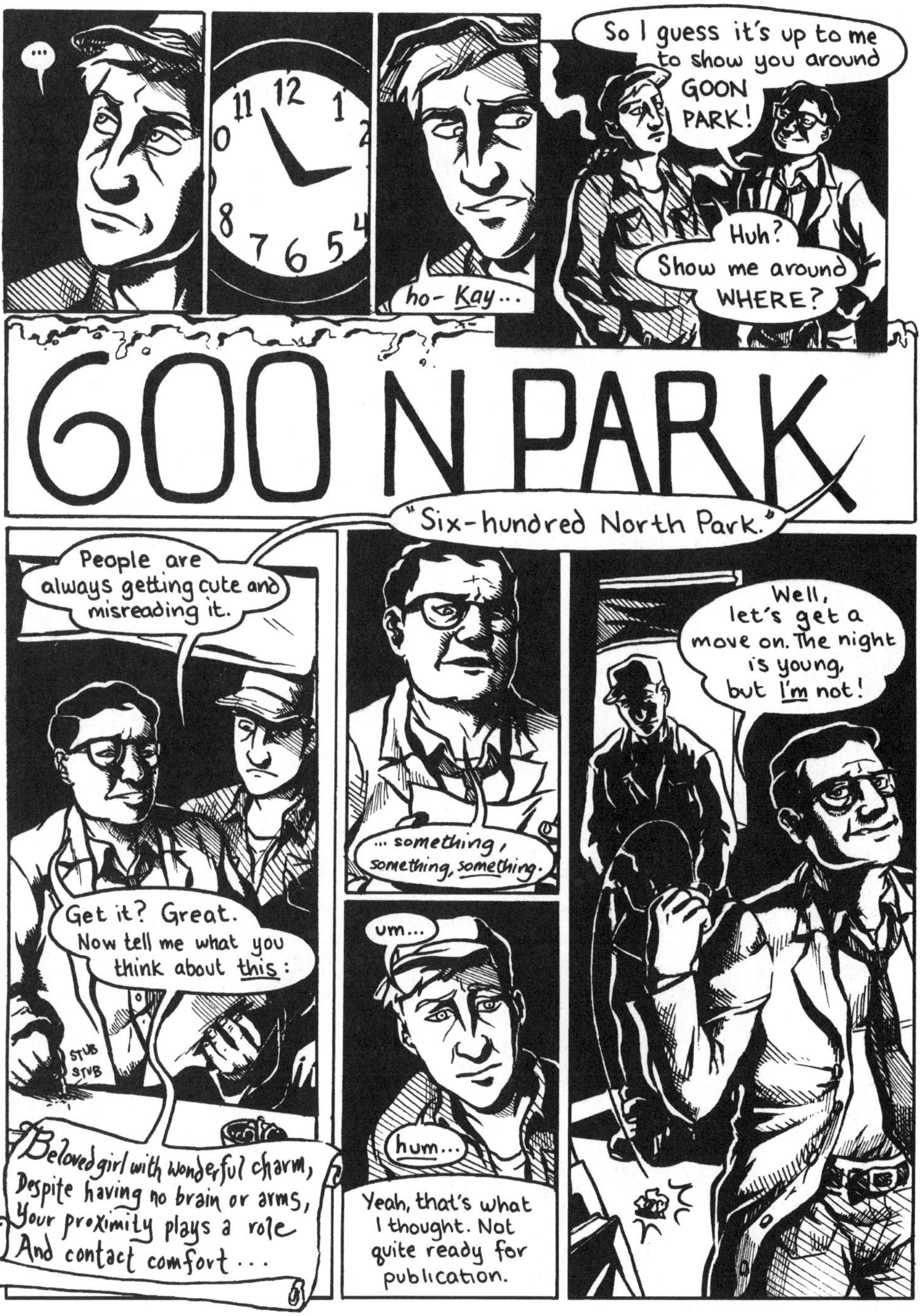
...
ho-Kay...
So I guess it's up to me to show you around GOON PARK!
Huh? Show me around WHERE?
600 N PARK
"Six-hundred North Park."
People are always getting cute and misreading it.
Get it? Great. Now tell me what you think about this:
STUB STUB
Beloved girl with wonderful charm,
Despite having no brain or arms,
Your proximity plays a role
And contact comfort ...
... something, something, something.
um...
hum...
Yeah, that's what I thought. Not quite ready for publication.
Well, let's get a move on. The night is young, but I'm not!

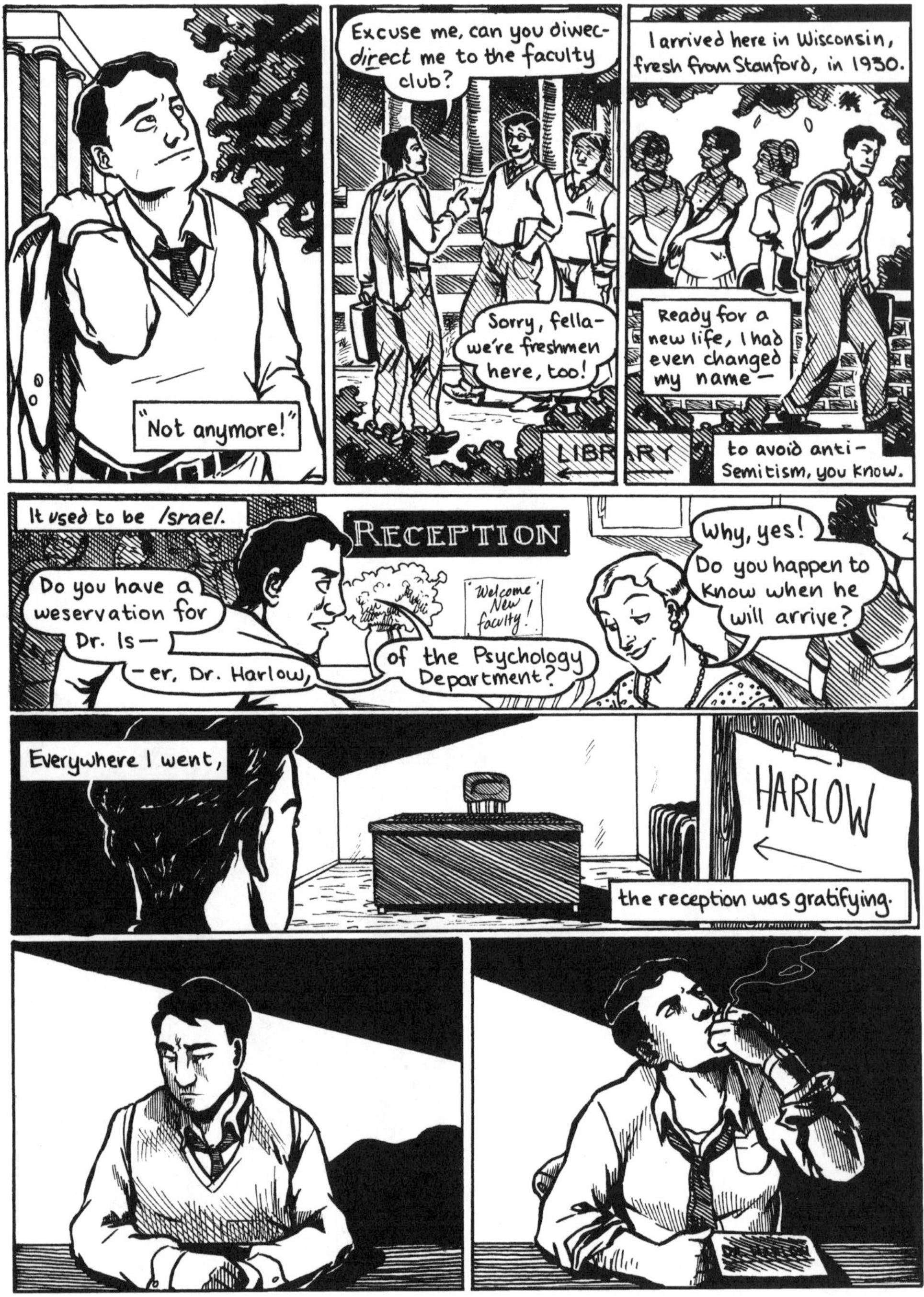
"Not anymore!"
Excuse me, can you diwec- direct me to the faculty club?
Sorry, fella- we're freshmen here, too!
LIBR ARY
I arrived here in Wisconsin, fresh from Stanford, in 1930.
Ready for a new life, I had even changed my name—
to avoid anti-Semitism, you know.
It used to be Israel.
RECEPTION
Do you have a weservation for Dr. Is—
—er, Dr. Harlow,
of the Psychology Department?
Welcome New faculty!
Why, yes!
Do you happen to know when he will arrive?
Everywhere I went,
HARLOW
the reception was gratifying.

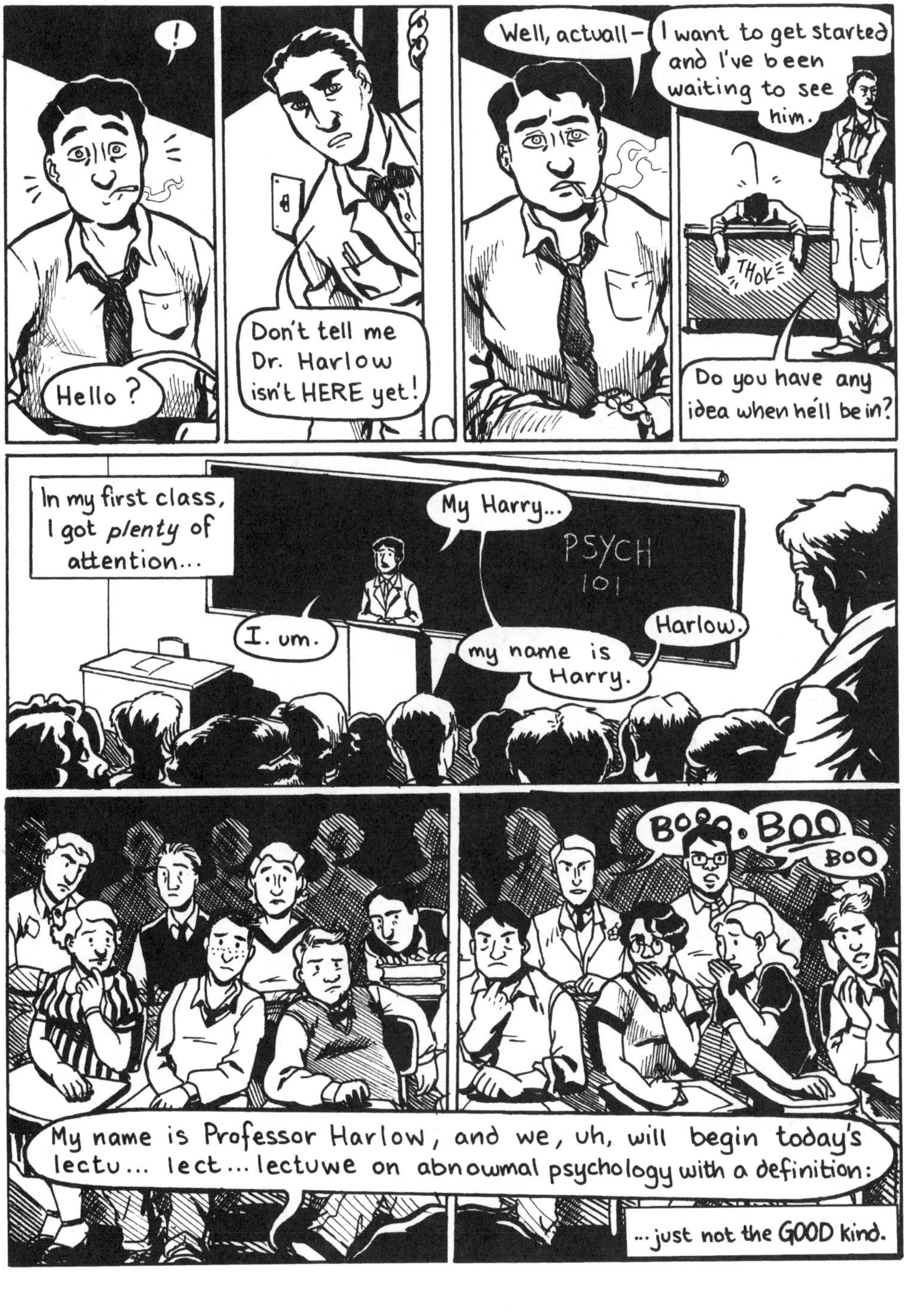
!
Hello?
Don't tell me Dr. Harlow isn't HERE yet!
Well, actuall–
I want to get started and I've been waiting to see him.
THOK
Do you have any idea when he'll be in?
In my first class, I got *plenty* of attention...
My Harry...
PSYCH 101
I. um.
my name is Harry.
Harlow.
BOO BOO BOO
BOO
My name is Professor Harlow, and we, uh, will begin today's lectu... lect... lectuwe on abnowmal psychology with a definition:
...just not the GOOD kind.

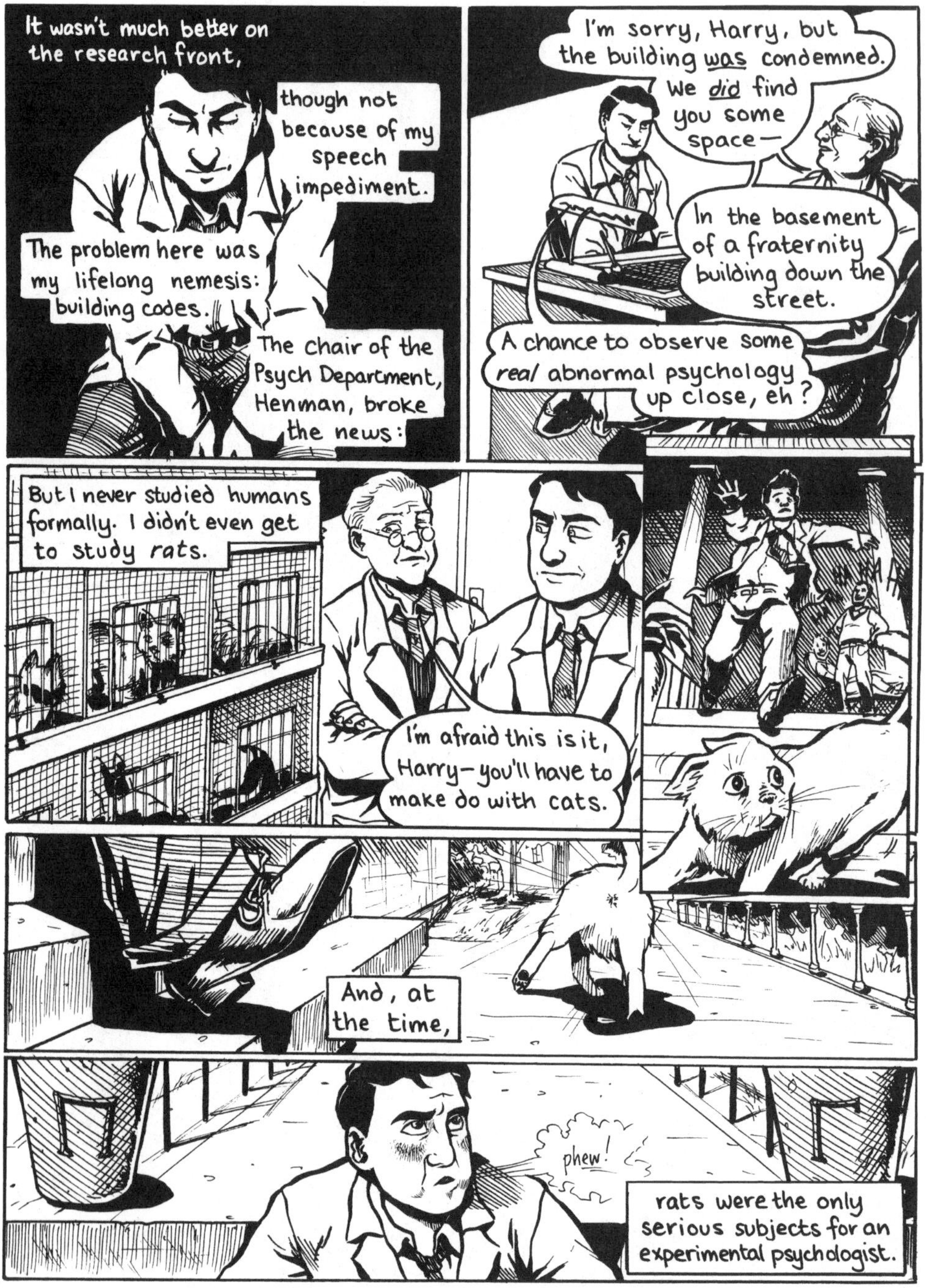
It wasn't much better on the research front,
though not because of my speech impediment.
The problem here was my lifelong nemesis: building codes.
The chair of the Psych Department, Henman, broke the news:
I'm sorry, Harry, but the building was condemned.
We did find you some space—
In the basement of a fraternity building down the street.
A chance to observe some real abnormal psychology up close, eh?
But I never studied humans formally. I didn't even get to study rats.
I'm afraid this is it, Harry—you'll have to make do with cats.
And, at the time,
phew!
rats were the only serious subjects for an experimental psychologist.

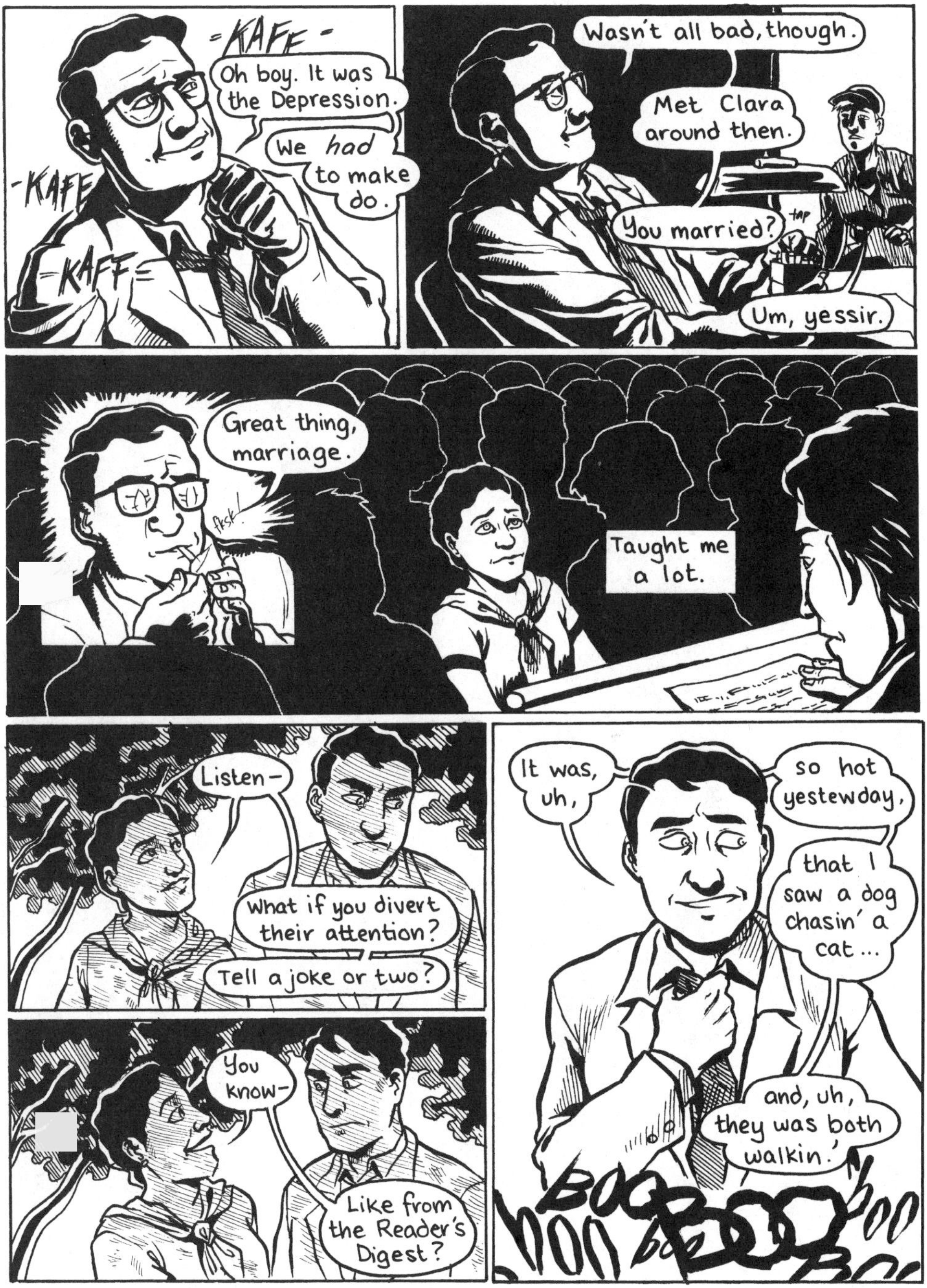
-KAFF-
Oh boy. It was the Depression.
-KAFF
We *had* to make do.
-KAFF=
Wasn't all bad, though.
Met Clara around then.
You married?
tap
Um, yessir.
Great thing, marriage.
Taught me a lot.
Listen–
What if you divert their attention?
Tell a joke or two?
You know–
Like from the Reader's Digest?
It was, uh,
so hot yestewday,
that I saw a dog chasin' a cat...
and, uh, they was both walkin.'
BOO
BOO
BOO

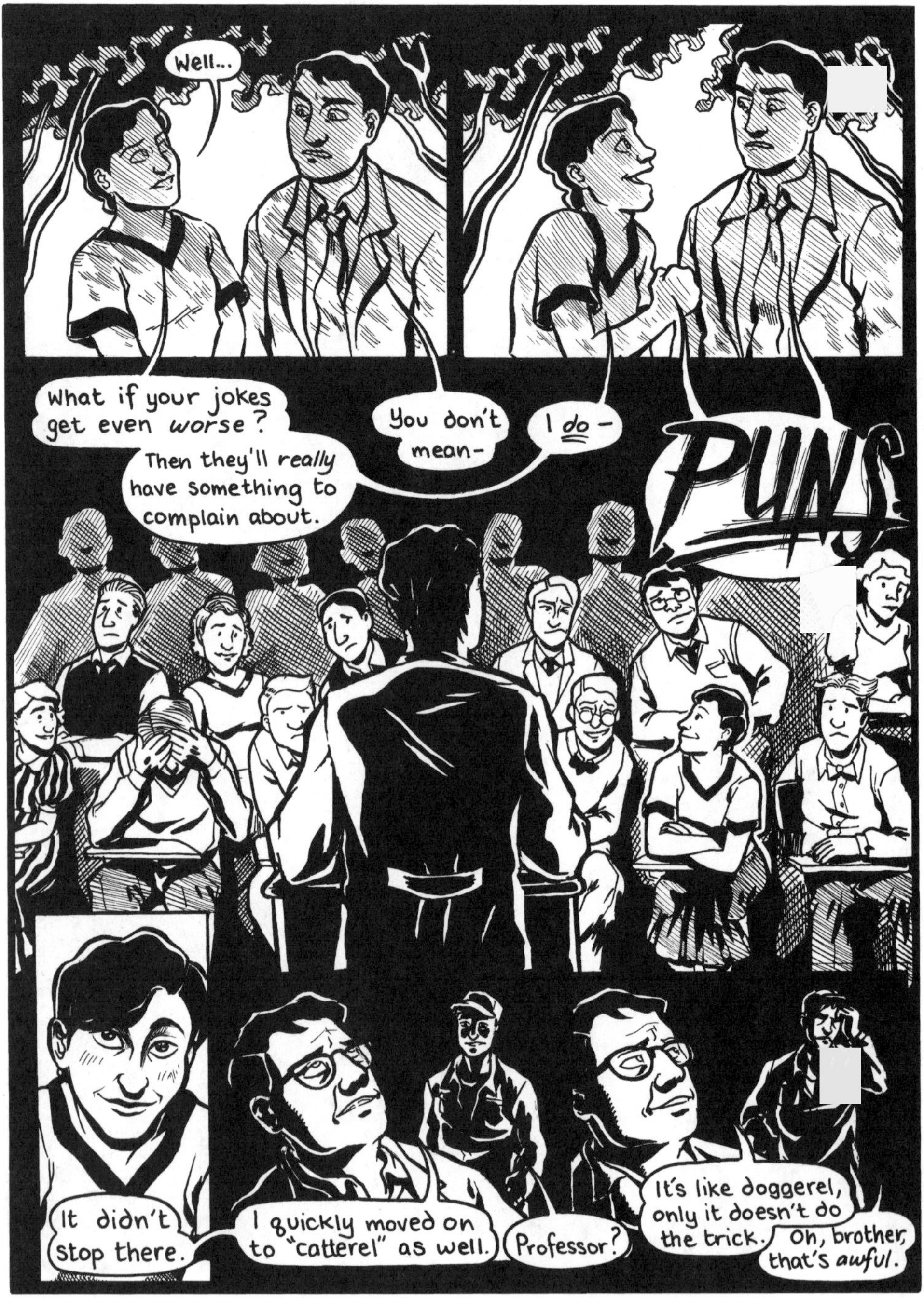
Well...
What if your jokes get even *worse*?
You don't mean-
I do-
Then they'll *really* have something to complain about.
PUNS
It didn't stop there.
I quickly moved on to "catterel" as well.
Professor?
It's like doggerel, only it doesn't do the trick.
Oh, brother, that's *awful*.

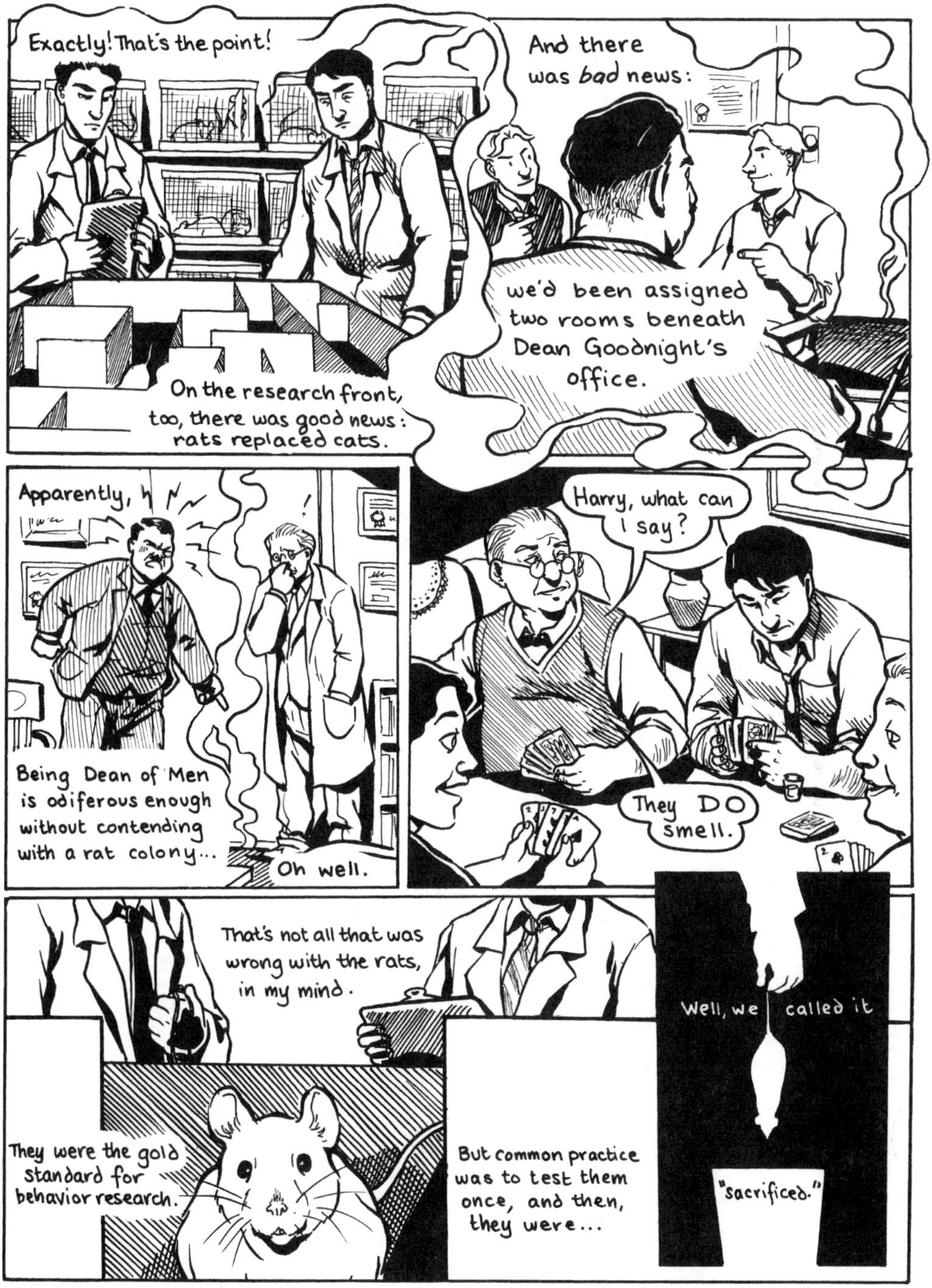
Exactly! That's the point!
On the research front, too, there was good news: rats replaced cats.
And there was *bad* news:
we'd been assigned two rooms beneath Dean Goodnight's office.
Apparently,
Being Dean of Men is odiferous enough without contending with a rat colony...
Oh well.
Harry, what can I say?
They DO smell.
That's not all that was wrong with the rats, in my mind.
They were the gold standard for behavior research.
But common practice was to test them once, and then, they were...
Well, we called it
"sacrificed."

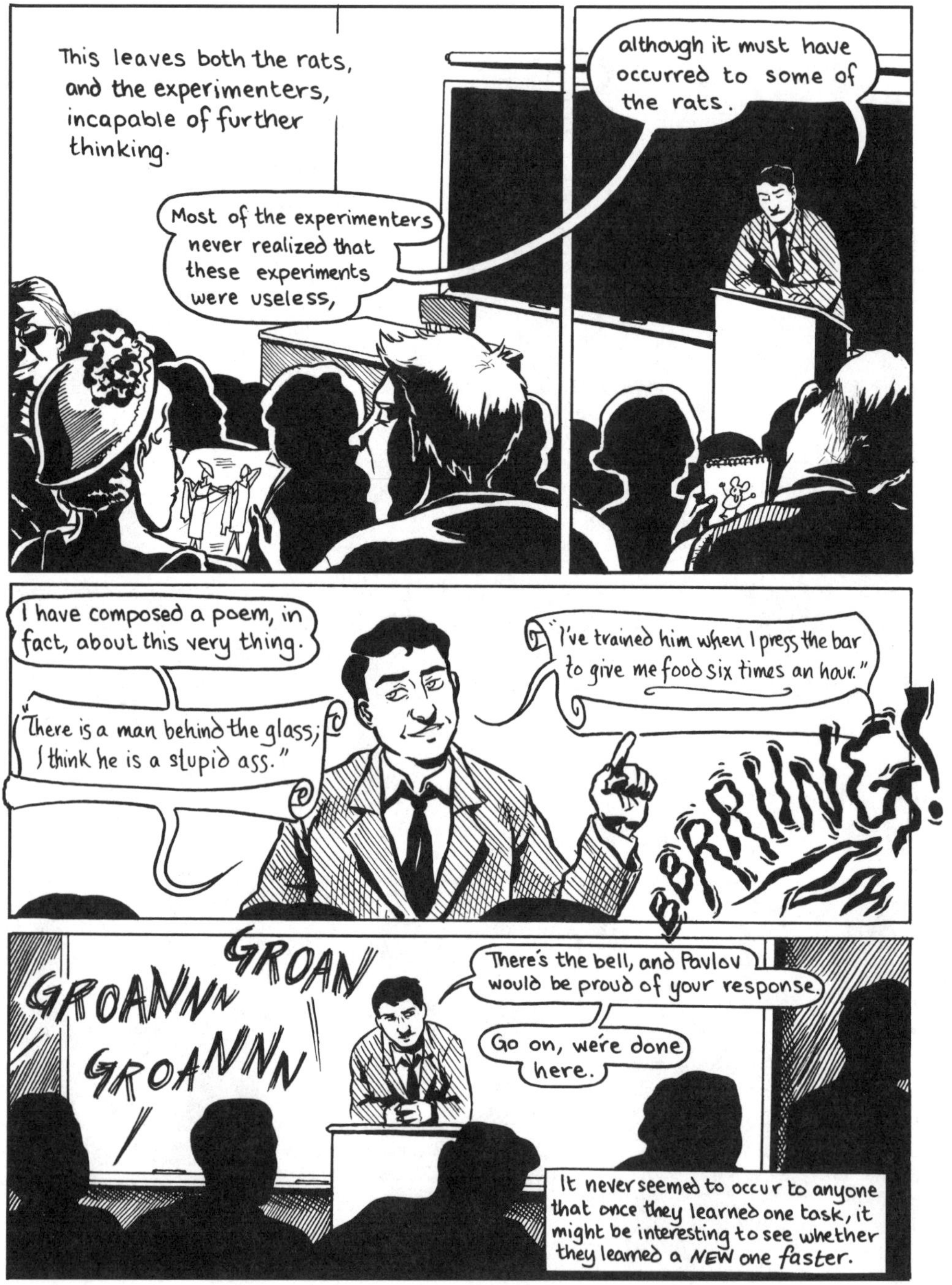
This leaves both the rats, and the experimenters, incapable of further thinking.
Most of the experimenters never realized that these experiments were useless,
although it must have occurred to some of the rats.
I have composed a poem, in fact, about this very thing.
"There is a man behind the glass; I think he is a stupid ass."
"I've trained him when I press the bar to give me food six times an hour."
BBRRING!
GROANNN
GROAN
GROANNN
There's the bell, and Pavlov would be proud of your response.
Go on, we're done here.
It never seemed to occur to anyone that once they learned one task, it might be interesting to see whether they learned a NEW one faster.

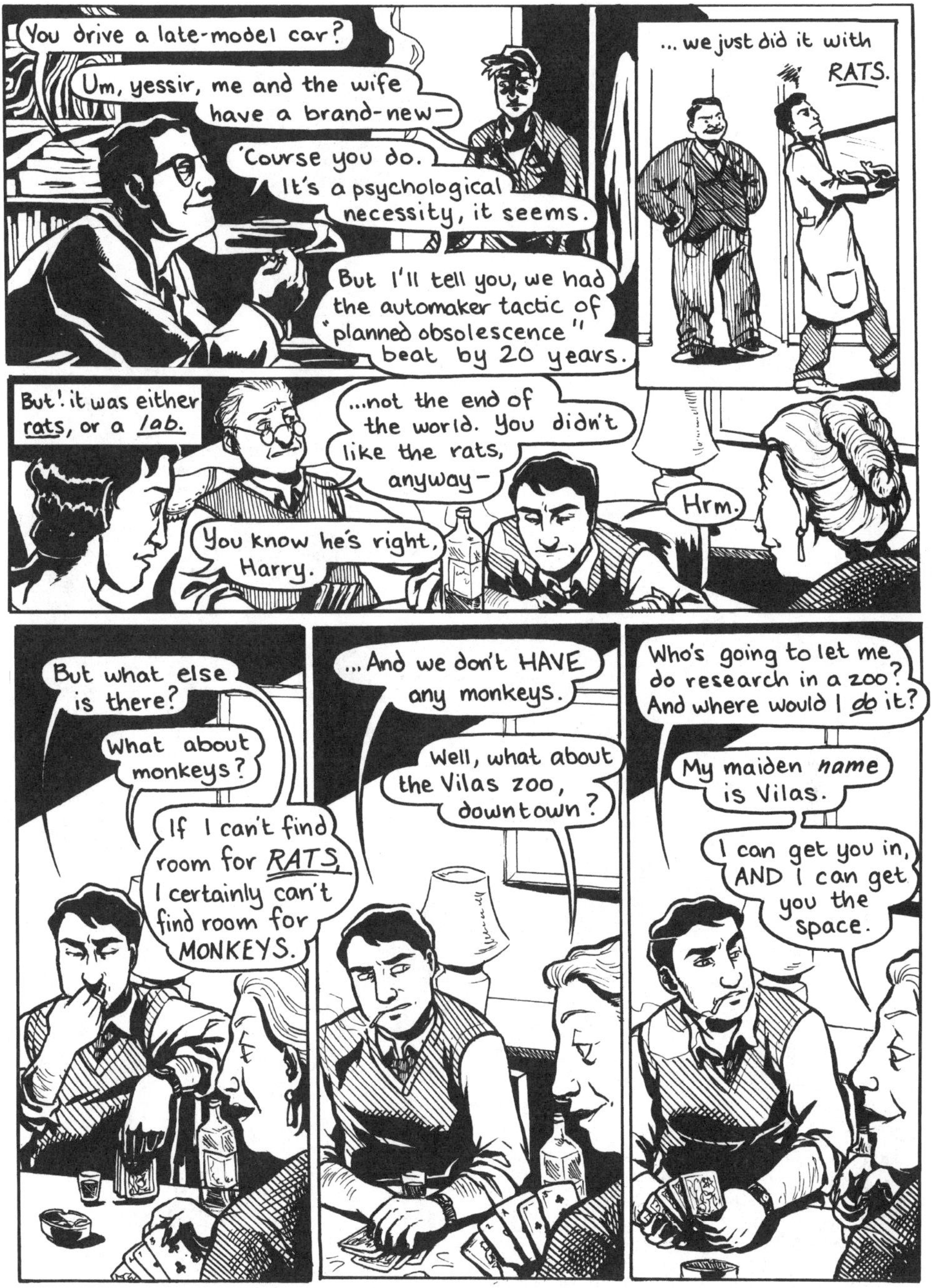
You drive a late-model car?
Um, yessir, me and the wife have a brand-new—
'Course you do. It's a psychological necessity, it seems.
But I'll tell you, we had the automaker tactic of "planned obsolescence" beat by 20 years.
... we just did it with RATS.
But! it was either rats, or a lab.
...not the end of the world. You didn't like the rats, anyway—
You know he's right, Harry.
Hrm.
But what else is there?
What about monkeys?
If I can't find room for RATS, I certainly can't find room for MONKEYS.
...And we don't HAVE any monkeys.
Well, what about the Vilas zoo, downtown?
Who's going to let me do research in a zoo? And where would I do it?
My maiden name is Vilas.
I can get you in, AND I can get you the space.

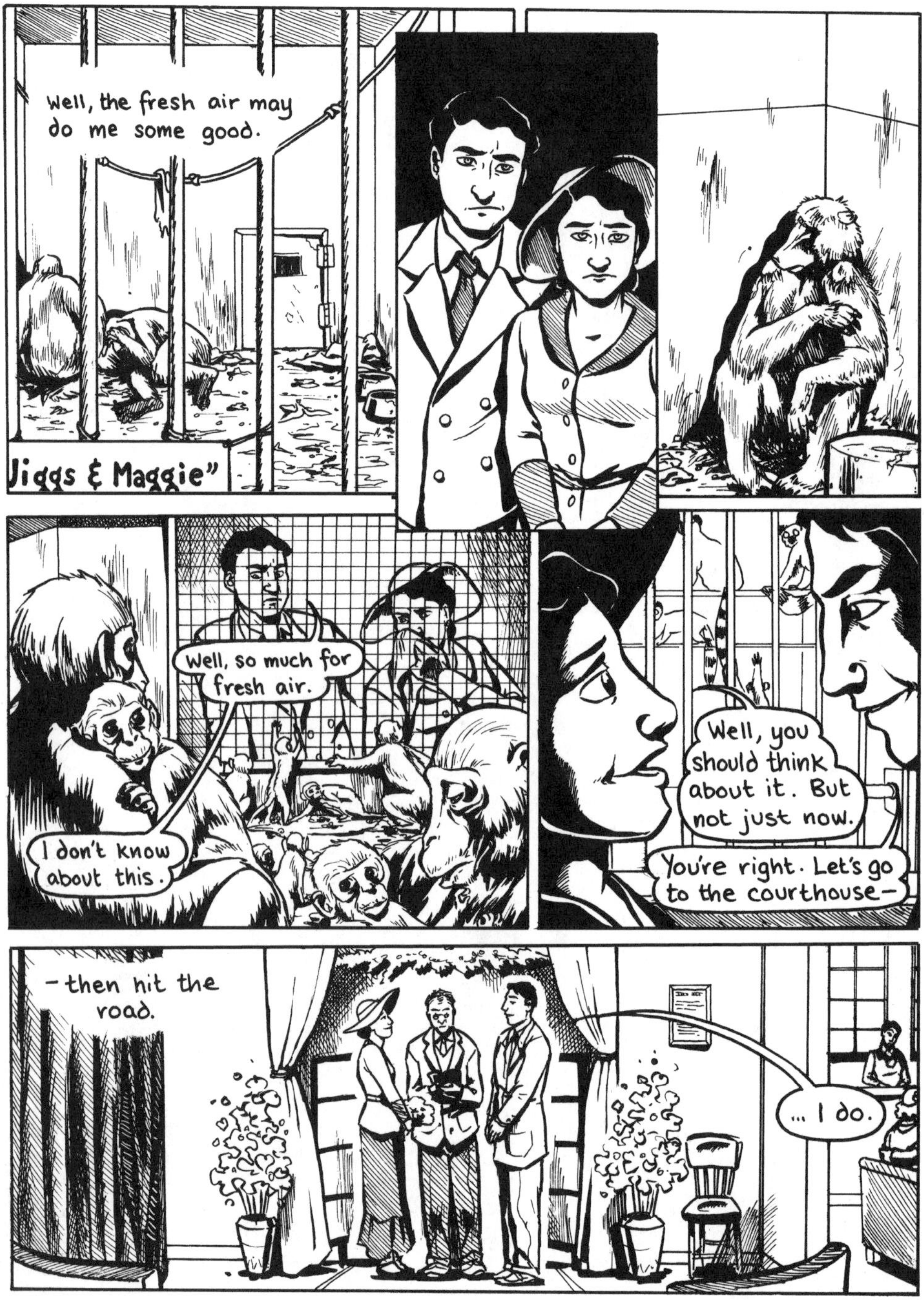
Well, the fresh air may do me some good.
Jiggs & Maggie"
Well, so much for fresh air.
I don't know about this.
Well, you should think about it. But not just now.
You're right. Let's go to the courthouse–
–then hit the road.
... I do.

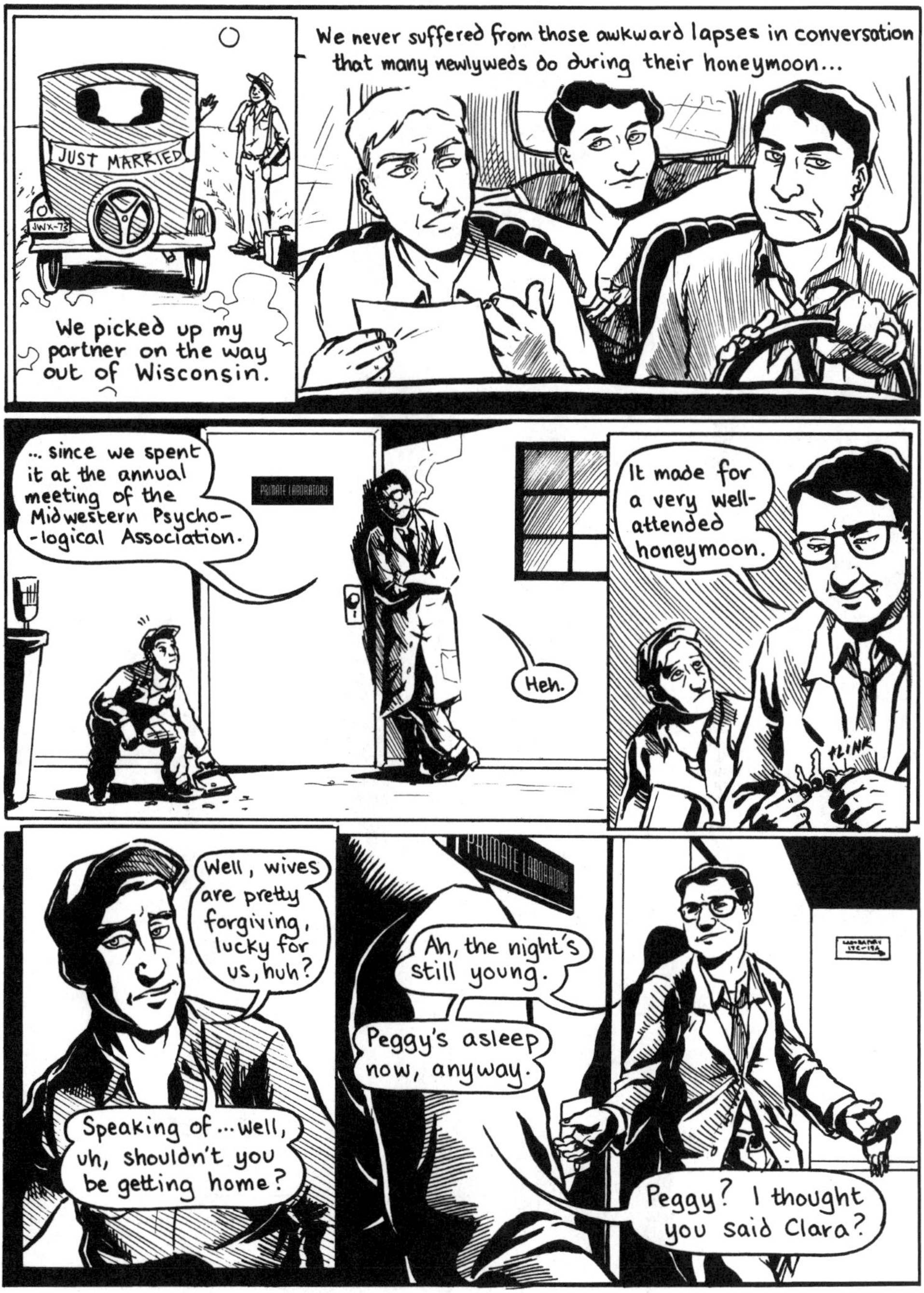
JUST MARRIED
JWX-73
We picked up my partner on the way out of Wisconsin.
We never suffered from those awkward lapses in conversation that many newlyweds do during their honeymoon...
... since we spent it at the annual meeting of the Midwestern Psycho--logical Association.
PRIMATE LABORATORY
Heh.
It made for a very well-attended honeymoon.
FLINK
Well, wives are pretty forgiving, lucky for us, huh?
Speaking of... well, uh, shouldn't you be getting home?
PRIMATE LABORATORY
Ah, the night's still young.
Peggy's asleep now, anyway.
Peggy? I thought you said Clara?

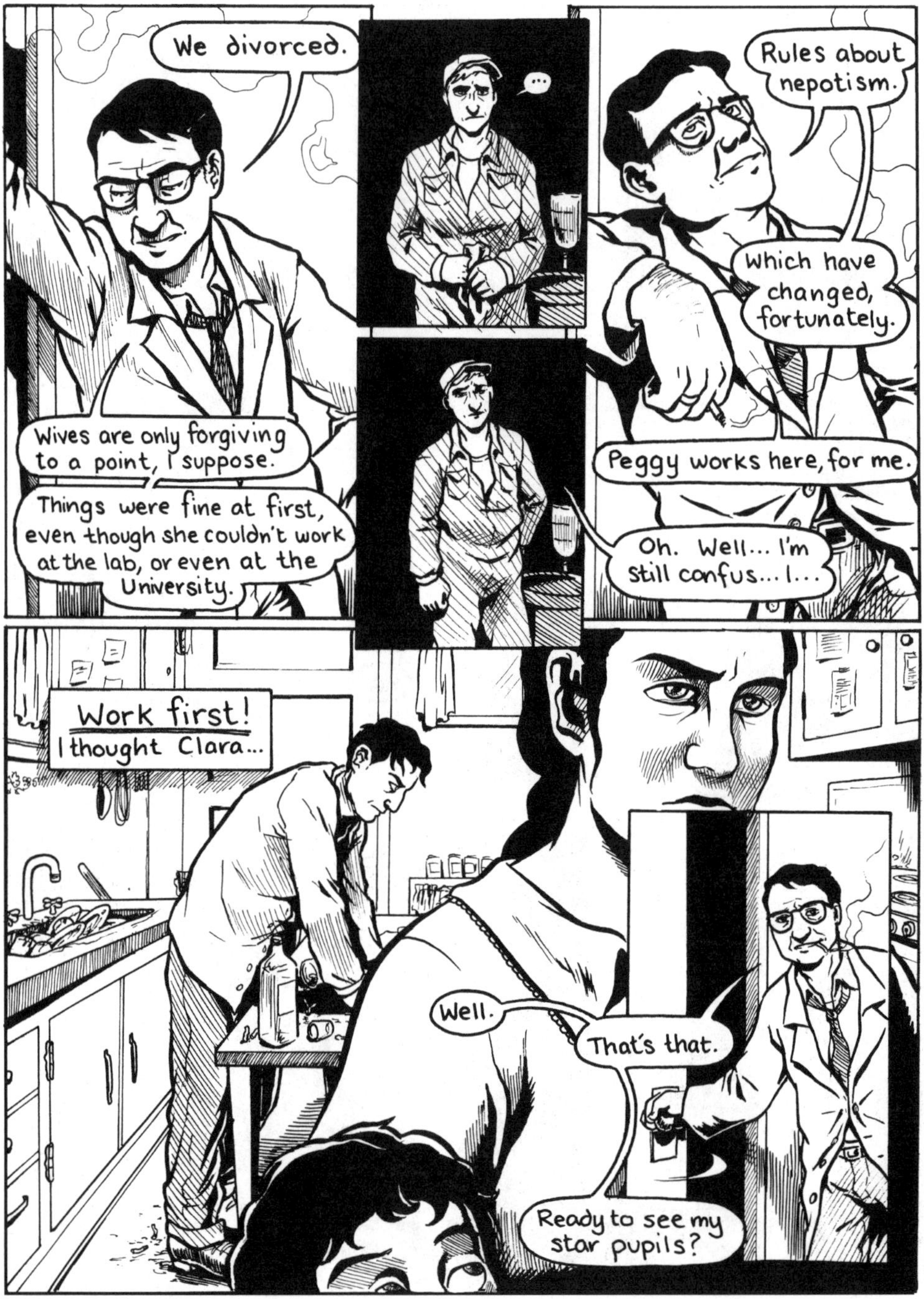
We divorced.
...
Rules about nepotism.
Which have changed, fortunately.
Wives are only forgiving to a point, I suppose.
Things were fine at first, even though she couldn't work at the lab, or even at the University.
Peggy works here, for me.
Oh. Well... I'm still confus... I...
Work first! I thought Clara...
Well.
That's that.
Ready to see my star pupils?

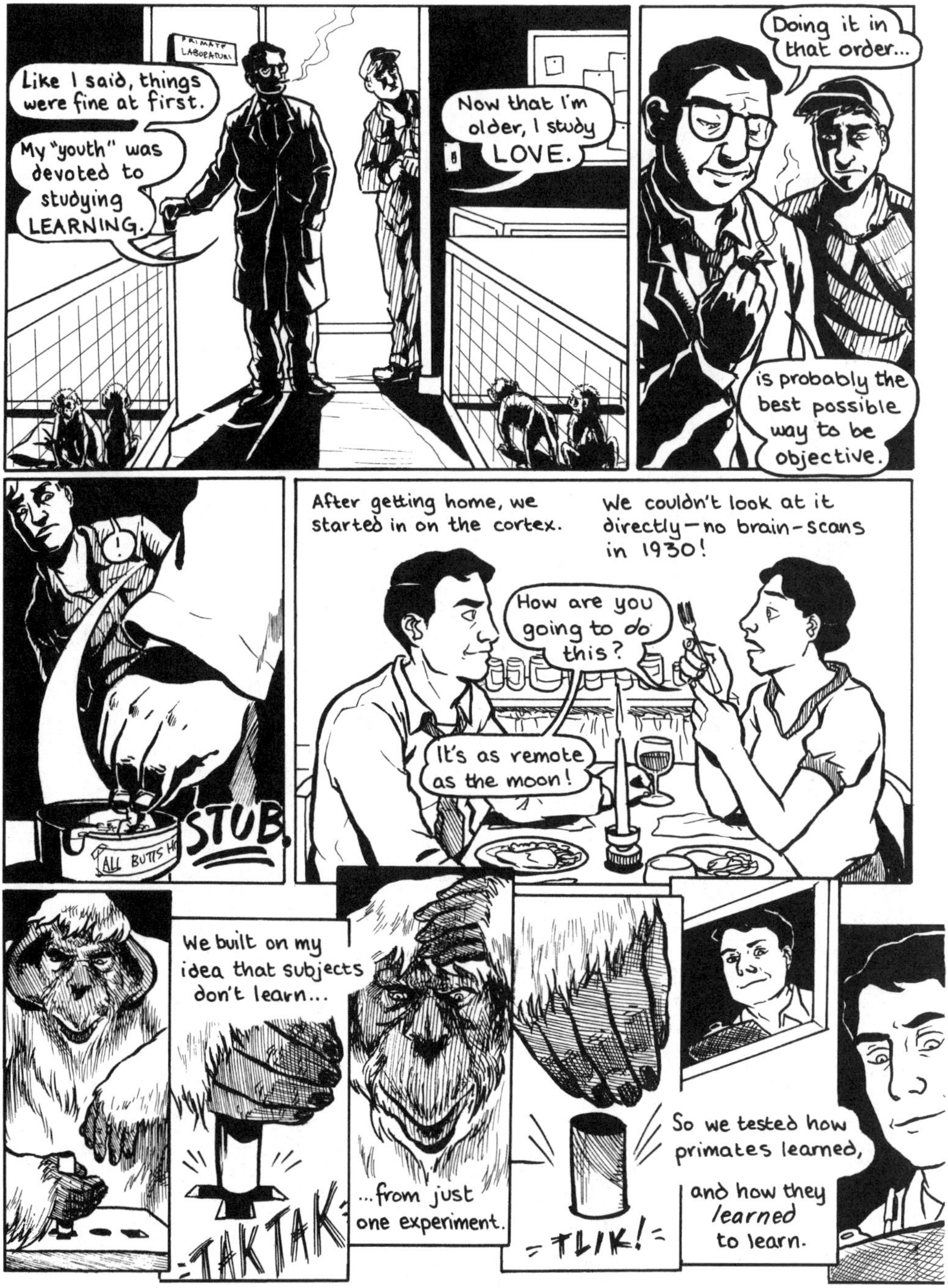
Like I said, things were fine at first.
My "youth" was devoted to studying LEARNING.
Now that I'm older, I study LOVE.
Doing it in that order...
is probably the best possible way to be objective.
STUB.
After getting home, we started in on the cortex.
We couldn't look at it directly—no brain-scans in 1930!
How are you going to do this?
It's as remote as the moon!
We built on my idea that subjects don't learn...
TAKTAK
...from just one experiment.
TLIK!
So we tested how primates learned,
and how they learned to learn.

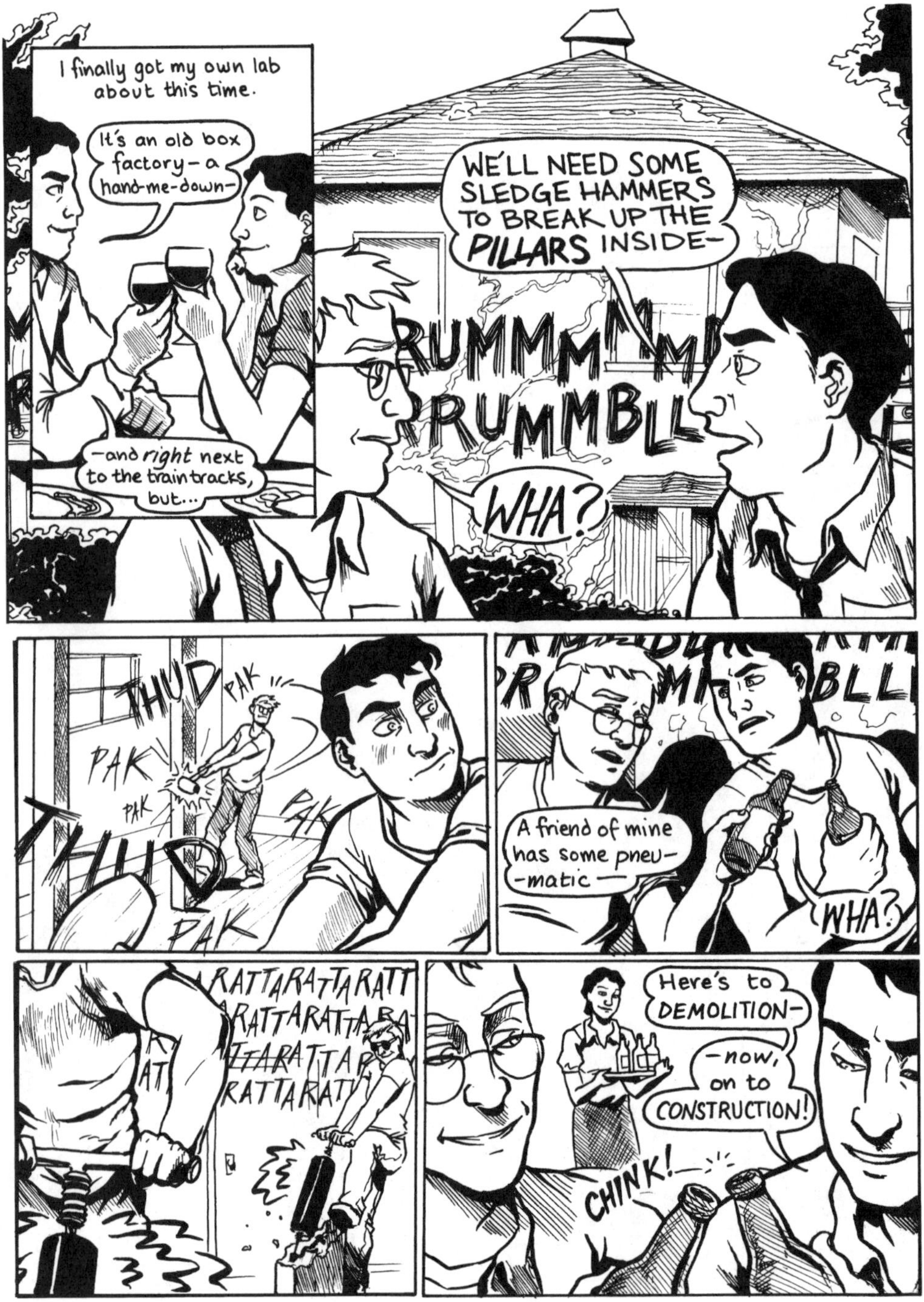
I finally got my own lab about this time.
It's an old box factory—a hand-me-down—
—and *right* next to the train tracks, but...
WE'LL NEED SOME SLEDGE HAMMERS TO BREAK UP THE *PILLARS* INSIDE—
RUMMBLL
WHA?
THUD
PAK
PAK
PAK
PAK
THUD
PAK
A friend of mine has some pneu-matic—
WHA?
Here's to DEMOLITION—
—now, on to CONSTRUCTION!
CHINK!

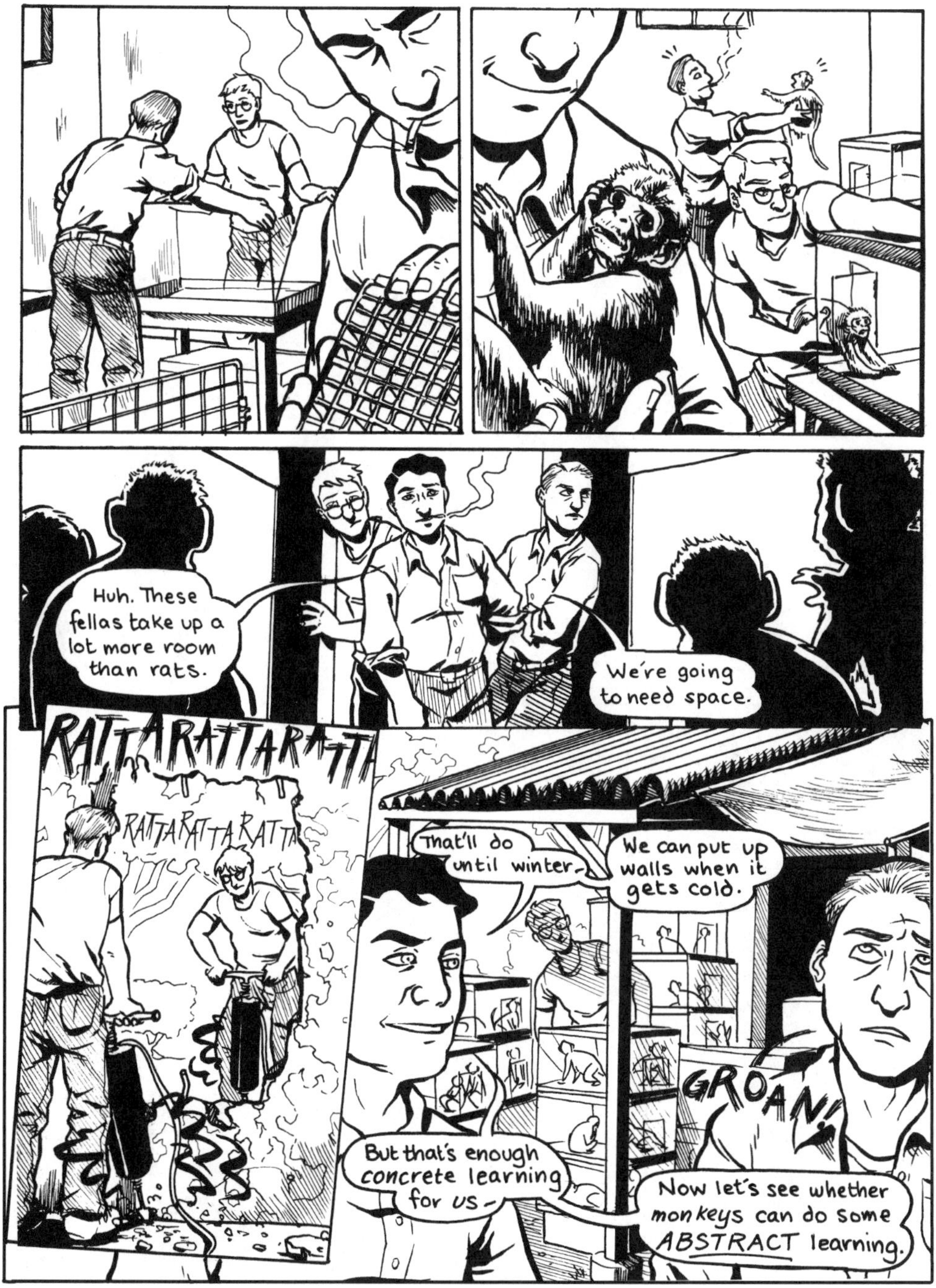
Huh. These fellas take up a lot more room than rats.
We're going to need space.
RATTARATTARATTA
RATTARATTARATTA
That'll do until winter.
We can put up walls when it gets cold.
GROAN!
But that's enough concrete learning for us.
Now let's see whether monkeys can do some ABSTRACT learning.

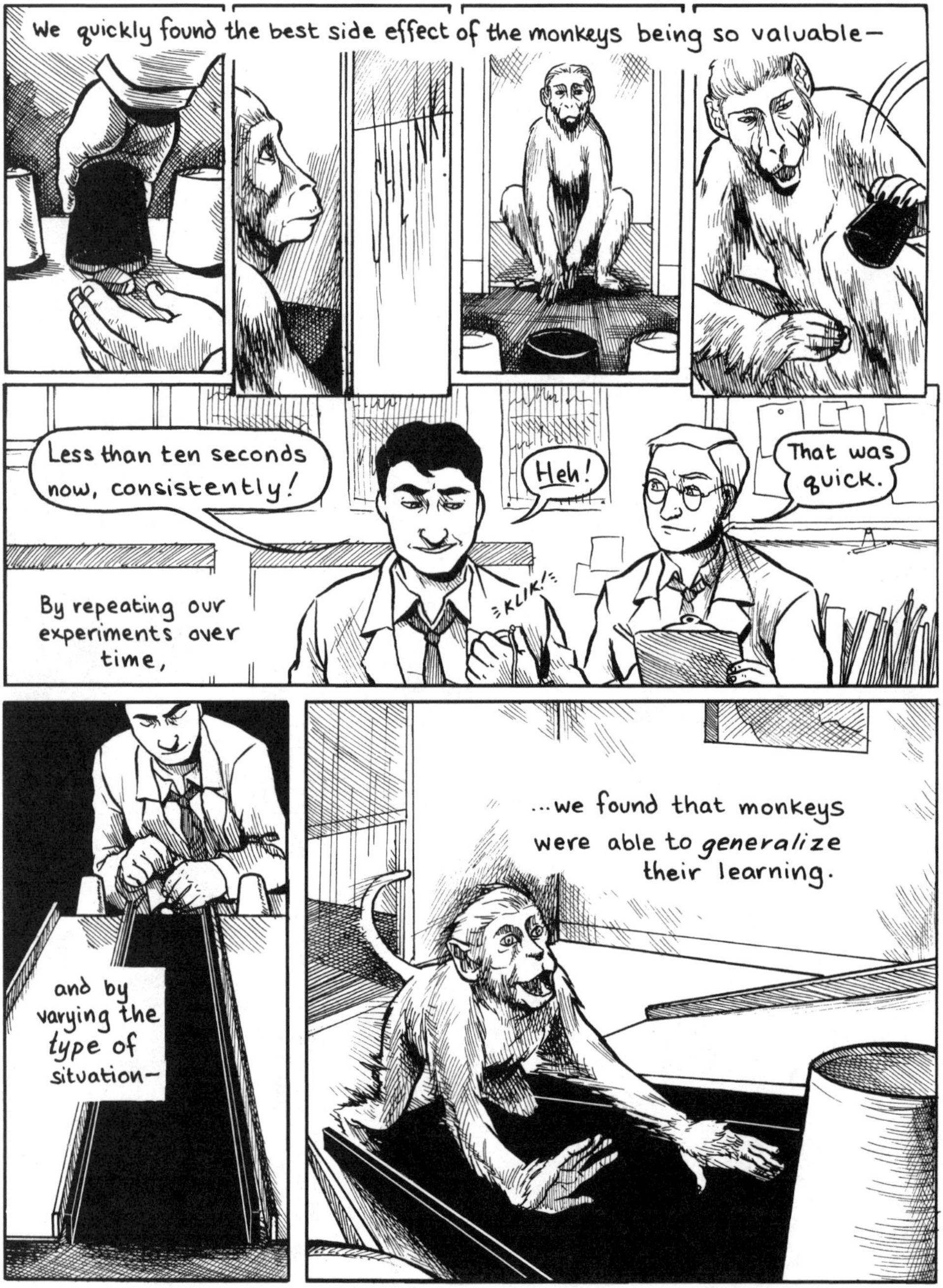
We quickly found the best side effect of the monkeys being so valuable—
Less than ten seconds now, consistently!
Heh!
That was quick.
KLIK!
By repeating our experiments over time,
and by varying the *type* of situation—
...we found that monkeys were able to *generalize* their learning.

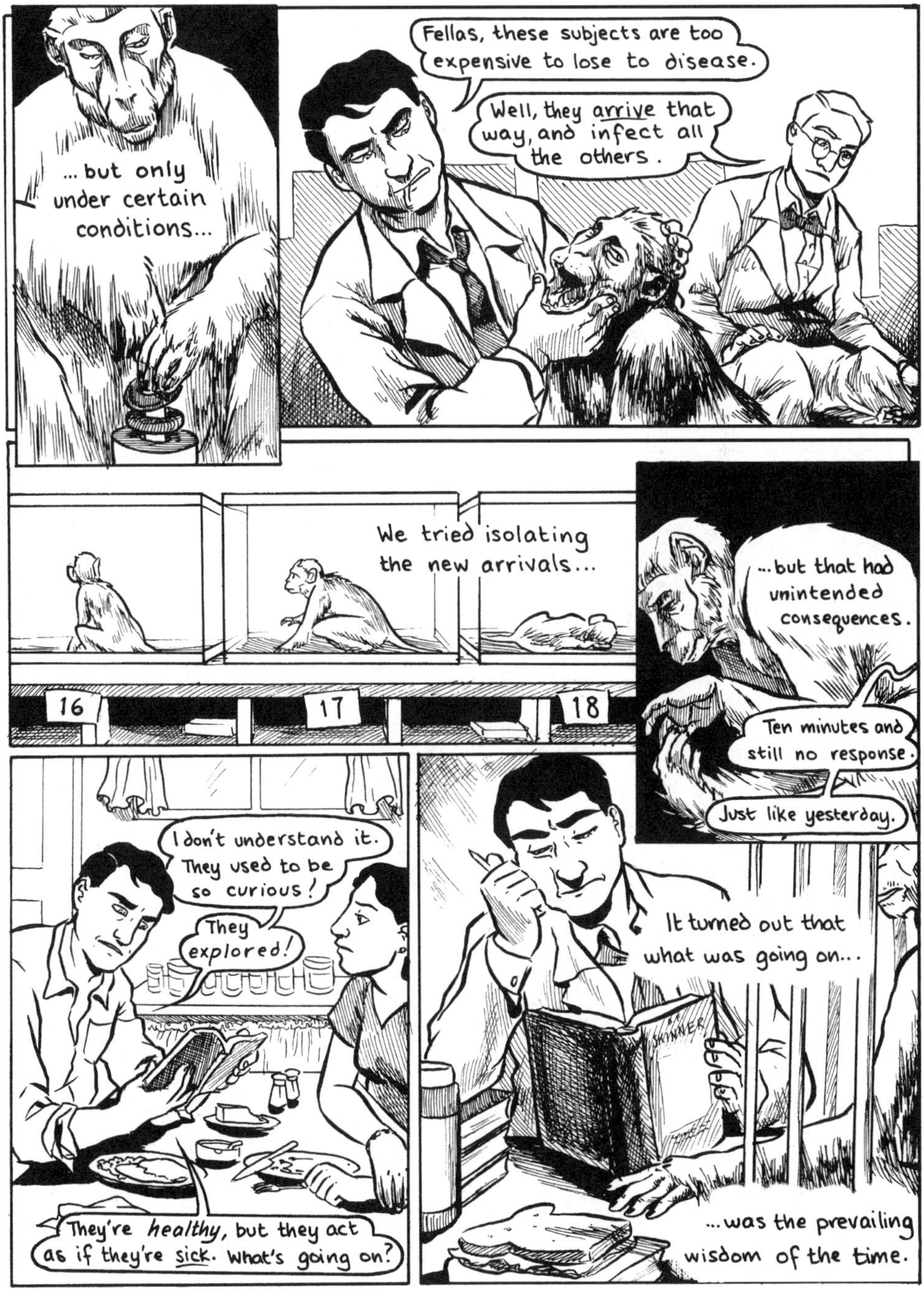
...but only under certain conditions...
Fellas, these subjects are too expensive to lose to disease.
Well, they arrive that way, and infect all the others.
We tried isolating the new arrivals...
16
17
18
...but that had unintended consequences.
Ten minutes and still no response.
Just like yesterday.
I don't understand it. They used to be so curious!
They explored!
They're healthy, but they act as if they're sick. What's going on?
It turned out that what was going on...
SKINNER
...was the prevailing wisdom of the time.

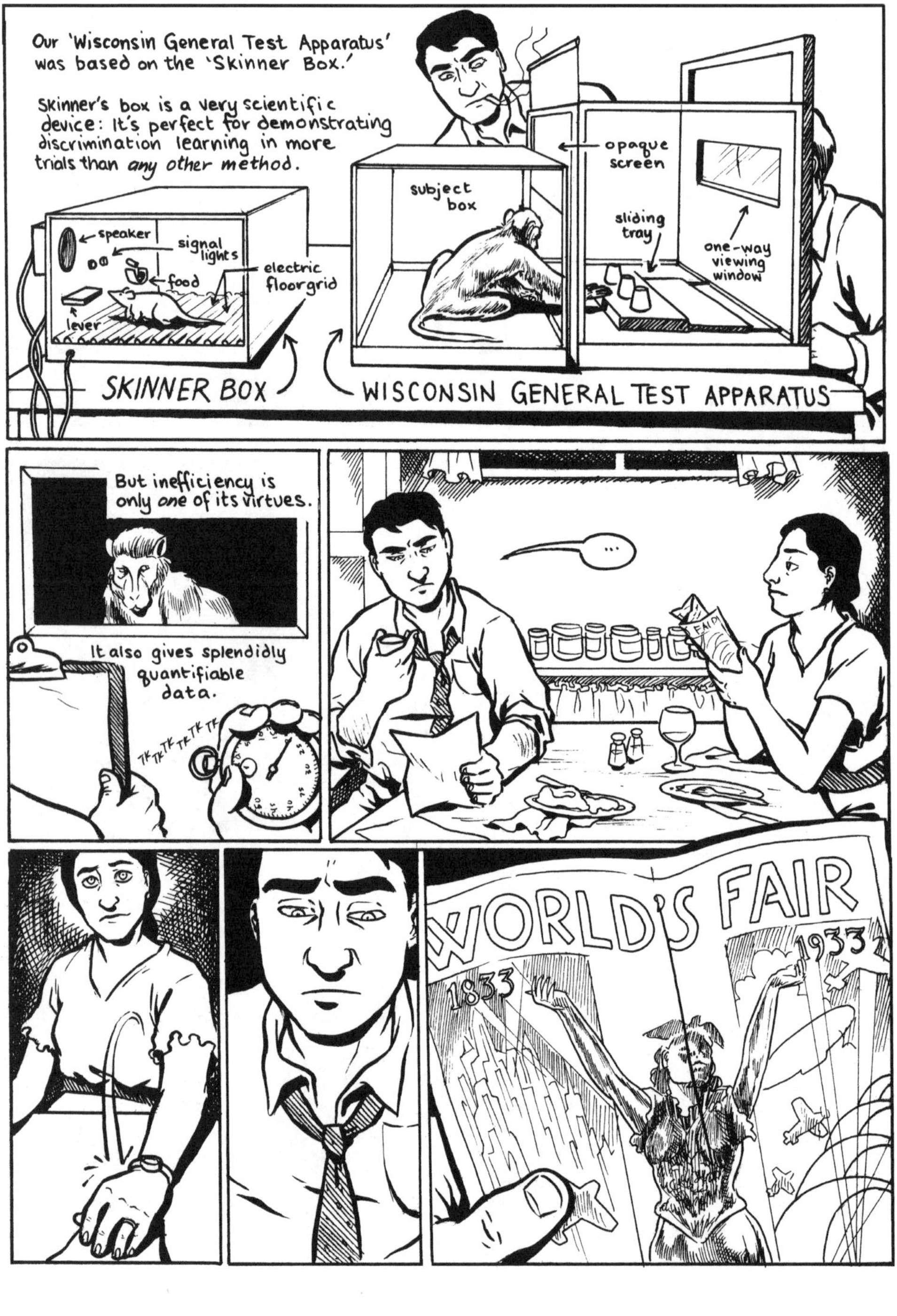
Our 'Wisconsin General Test Apparatus' was based on the 'Skinner Box.'
Skinner's box is a very scientific device: It's perfect for demonstrating discrimination learning in more trials than *any other method*.
speaker
signal lights
food
electric floorgrid
lever
subject box
opaque screen
sliding tray
one-way viewing window
SKINNER BOX
WISCONSIN GENERAL TEST APPARATUS
But inefficiency is only *one* of its virtues.
It also gives splendidly quantifiable data.
TK TK TK TK TK TK
...
WORLD'S FAIR
1833
1933

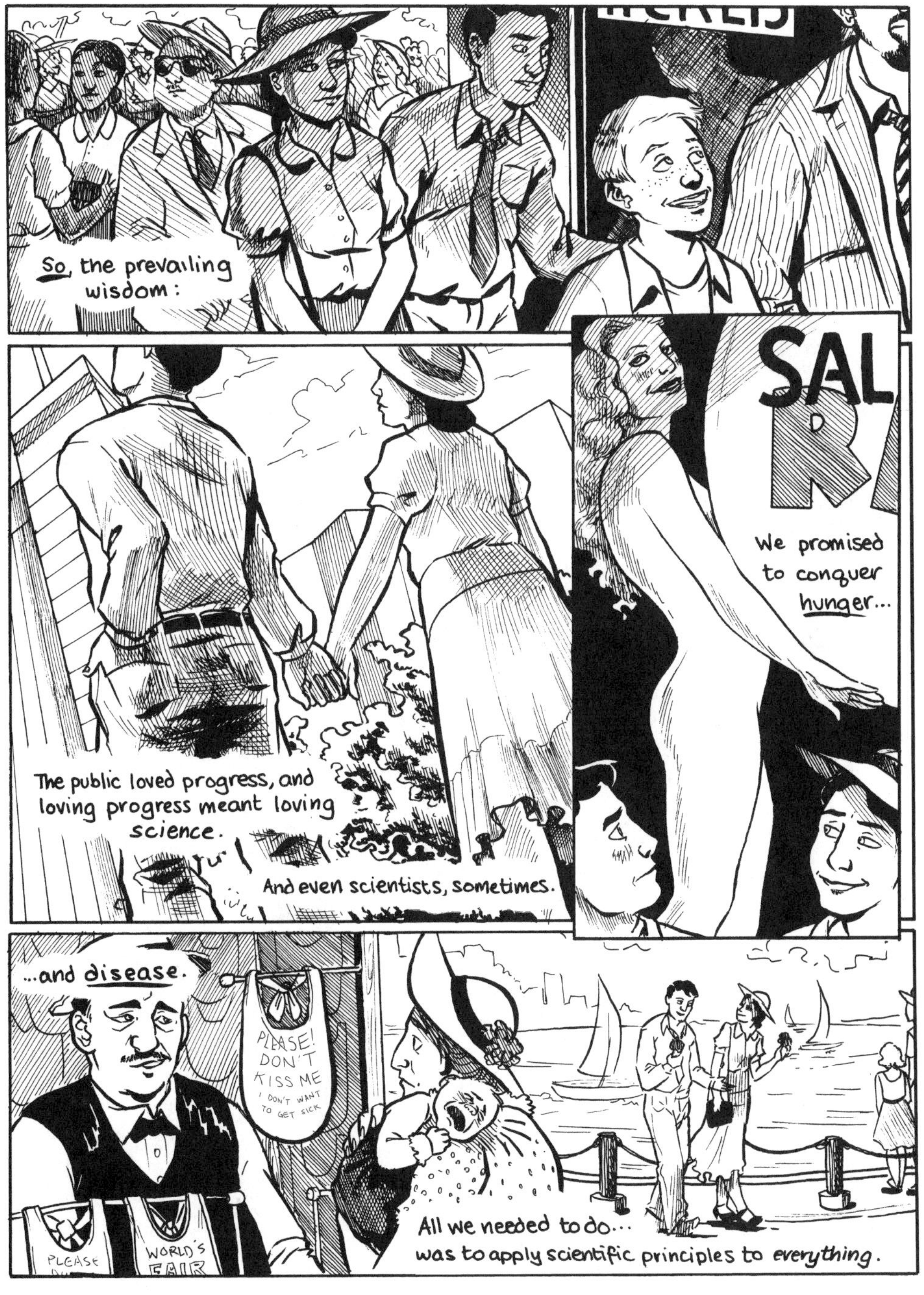
So, the prevailing wisdom:
The public loved progress, and loving progress meant loving science.
And even scientists, sometimes.
SAL
We promised to conquer hunger...
...and disease.
PLEASE! DON'T KISS ME
I DON'T WANT TO GET SICK
PLEASE
WORLD'S FAIR
All we needed to do... was to apply scientific principles to everything.

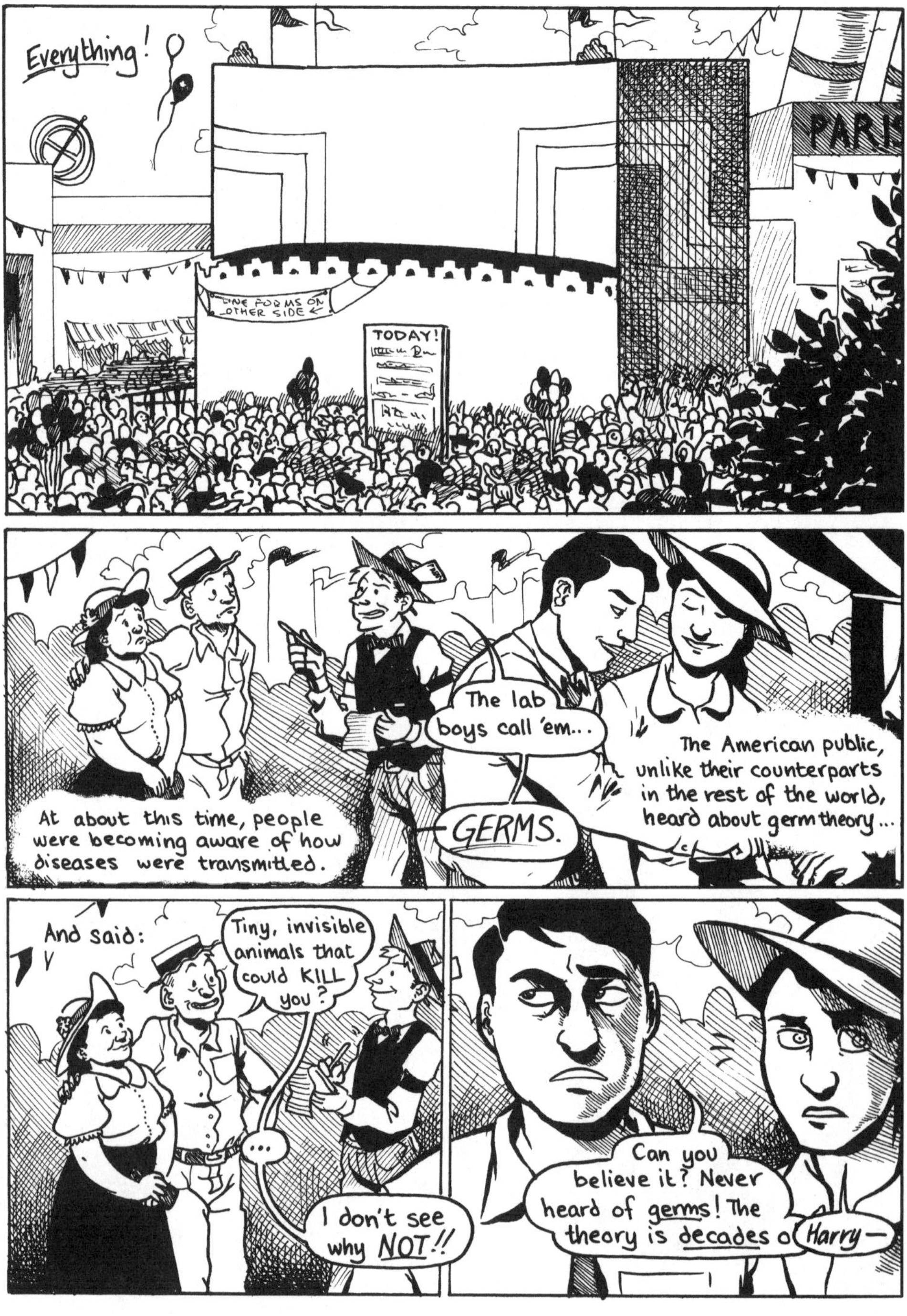
Everything!
LINE FORMS ON OTHER SIDE
TODAY!
PARIS
At about this time, people were becoming aware of how diseases were transmitted.
The lab boys call 'em...
GERMS.
The American public, unlike their counterparts in the rest of the world, heard about germ theory...
And said:
Tiny, invisible animals that could KILL you?
...
I don't see why NOT!!
Can you believe it? Never heard of germs! The theory is decades o
Harry—

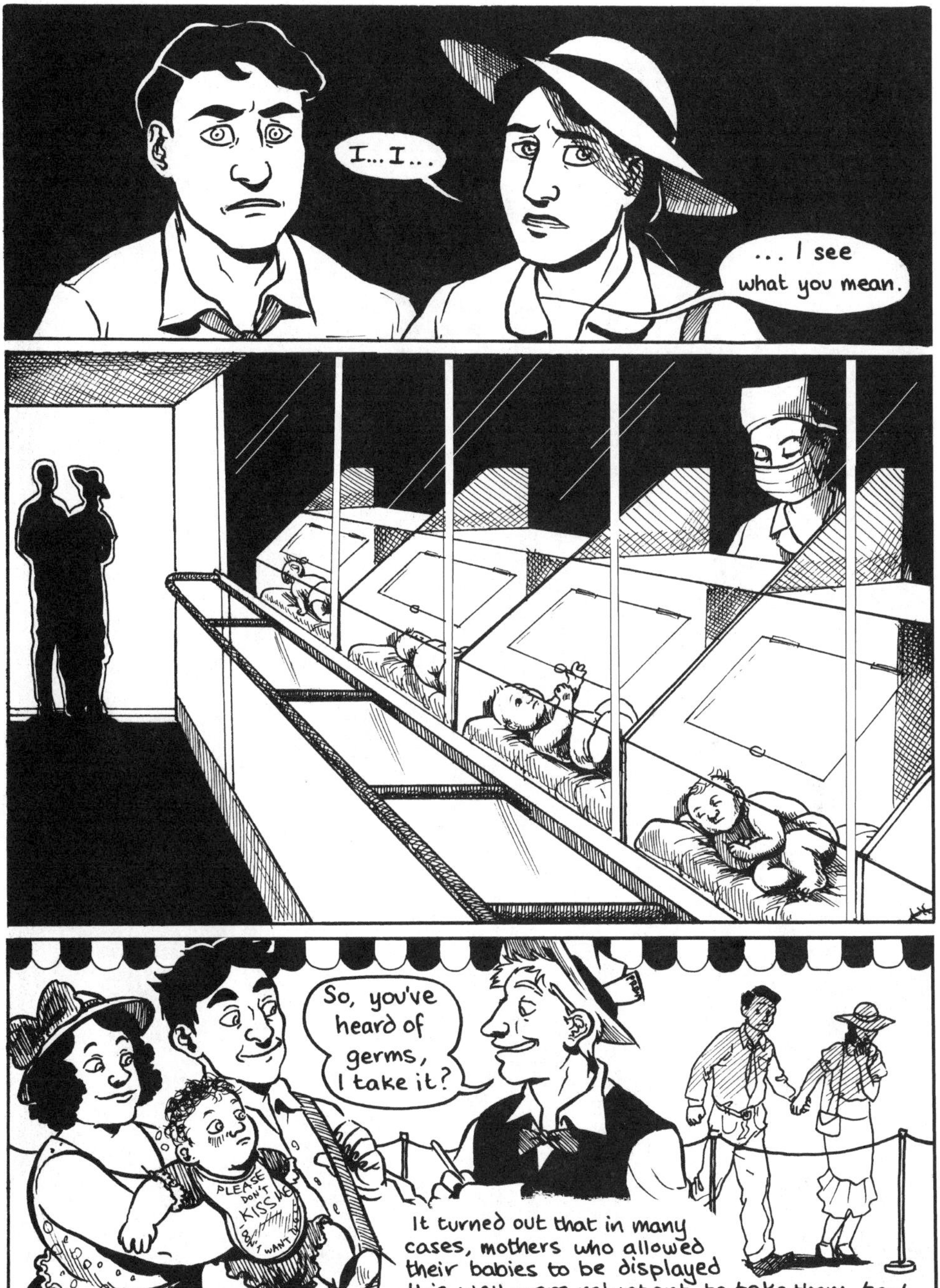
I... I...
... I see what you mean.
PLEASE DON'T KISS ME
So, you've heard of germs, I take it?
It turned out that in many cases, mothers who allowed their babies to be displayed this way were reluctant to take them *back*.

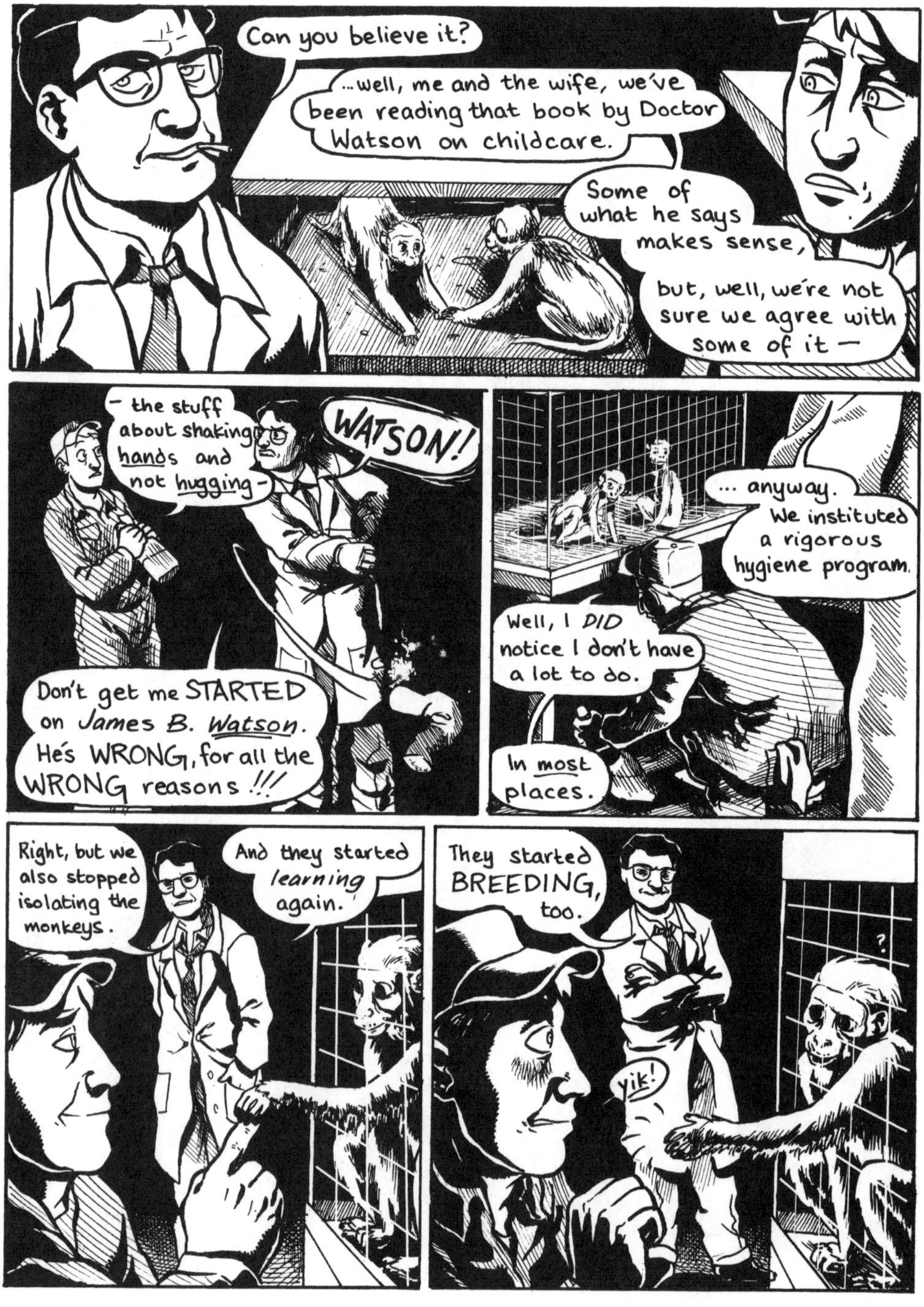
Can you believe it?
...well, me and the wife, we've been reading that book by Doctor Watson on childcare.
Some of what he says makes sense,
but, well, we're not sure we agree with some of it —
— the stuff about shaking hands and not hugging —
WATSON!
Don't get me STARTED on James B. Watson. He's WRONG, for all the WRONG reasons !!!
... anyway. We instituted a rigorous hygiene program.
Well, I DID notice I don't have a lot to do.
In most places.
Right, but we also stopped isolating the monkeys.
And they started learning again.
They started BREEDING, too.
yik!
?

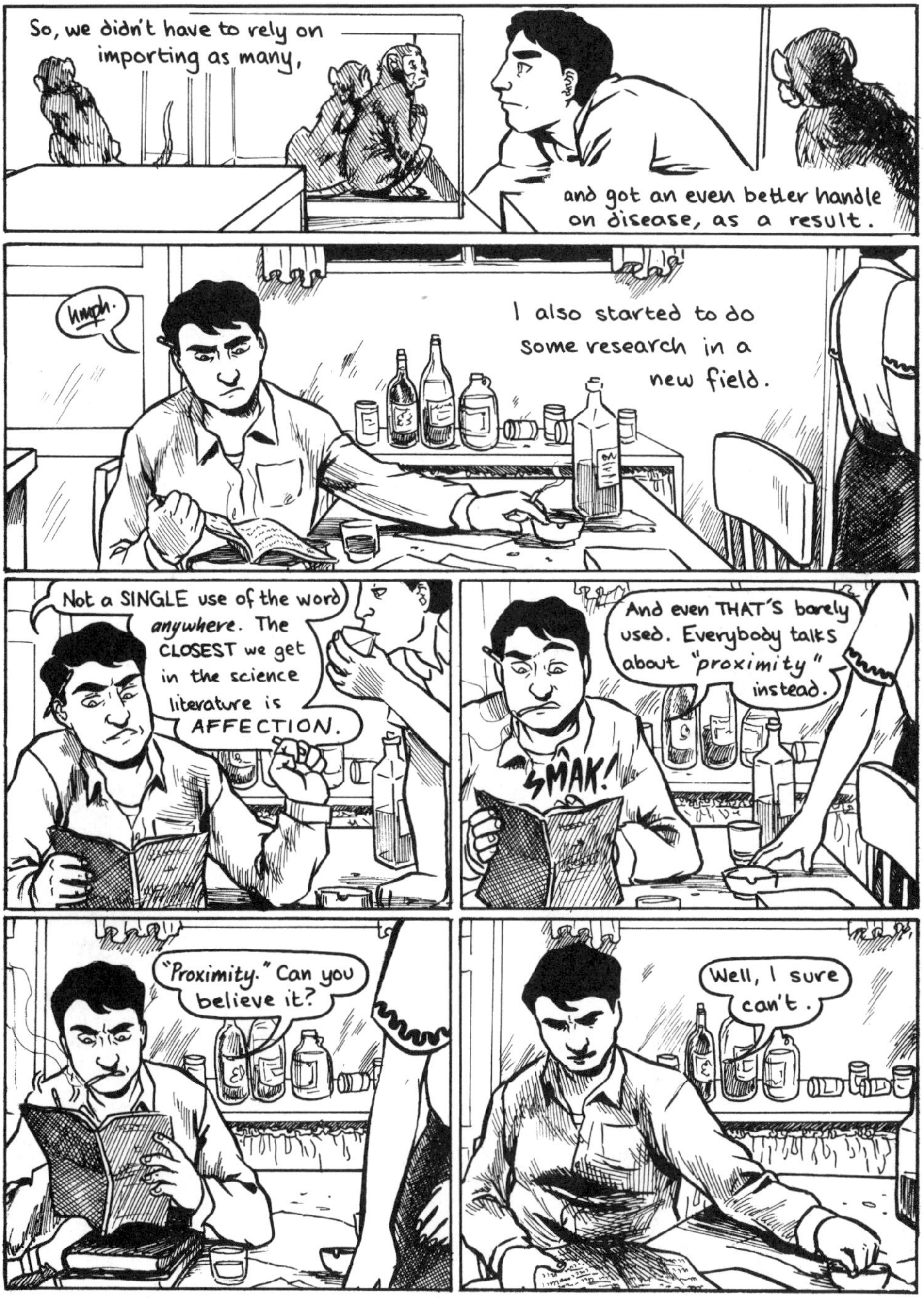
So, we didn't have to rely on importing as many,
and got an even better handle on disease, as a result.
hmph.
I also started to do some research in a new field.
Not a SINGLE use of the word *anywhere*. The CLOSEST we get in the science literature is AFFECTION.
And even THAT'S barely used. Everybody talks about "proximity" instead.
SMAK!
"Proximity." Can you believe it?
Well, I sure can't.

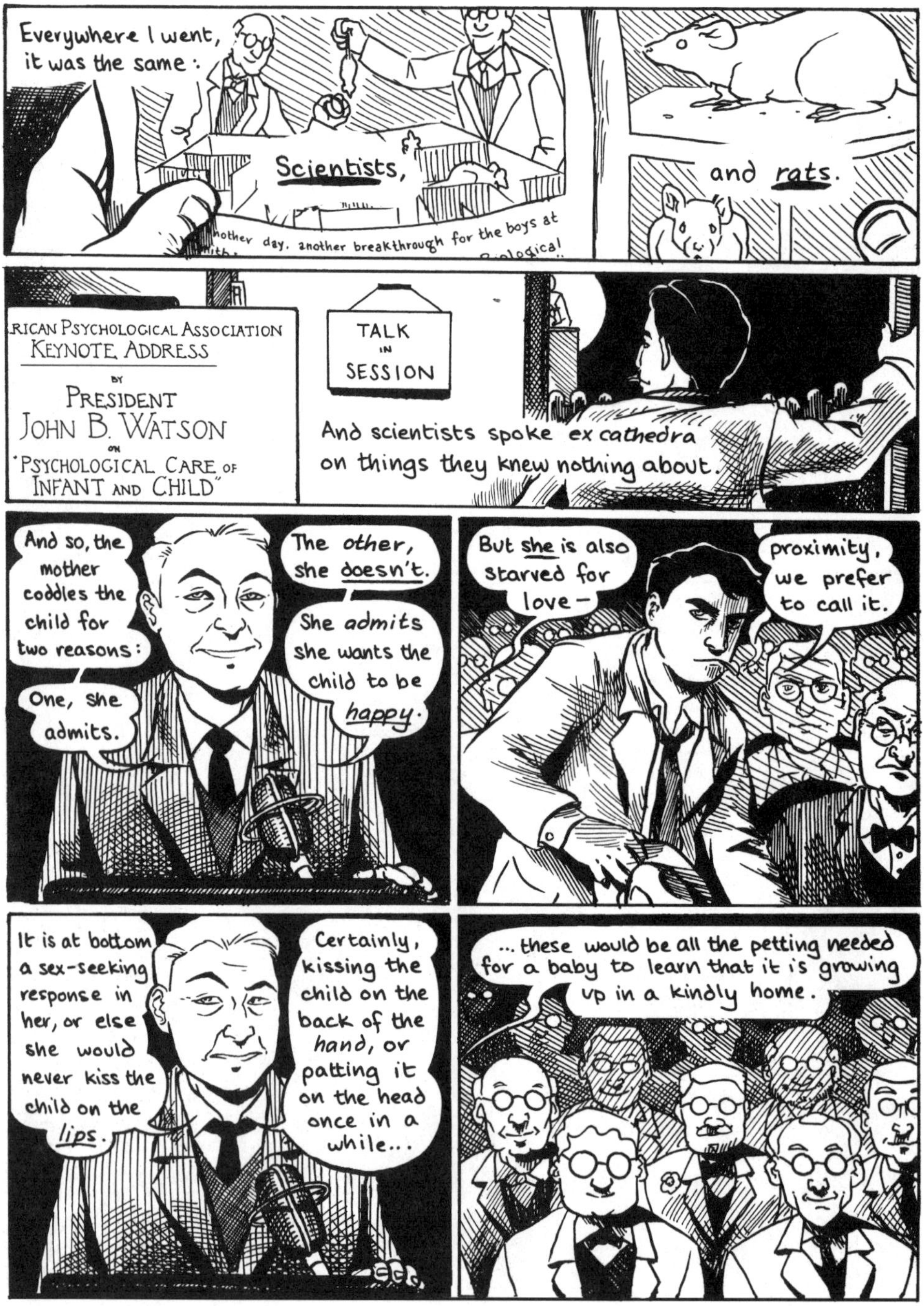
Everywhere I went, it was the same:
Scientists,
nother day. another breakthrough for the boys at
and rats.
RICAN PSYCHOLOGICAL ASSOCIATION
KEYNOTE ADDRESS
BY
PRESIDENT
JOHN B. WATSON
ON
"PSYCHOLOGICAL CARE OF INFANT AND CHILD"
TALK IN SESSION
And scientists spoke ex cathedra on things they knew nothing about.
And so, the mother coddles the child for two reasons:
One, she admits.
The other, she doesn't.
She admits she wants the child to be happy.
But she is also starved for love—
proximity, we prefer to call it.
It is at bottom a sex-seeking response in her, or else she would never kiss the child on the lips.
Certainly, kissing the child on the back of the hand, or patting it on the head once in a while...
...these would be all the petting needed for a baby to learn that it is growing up in a kindly home.

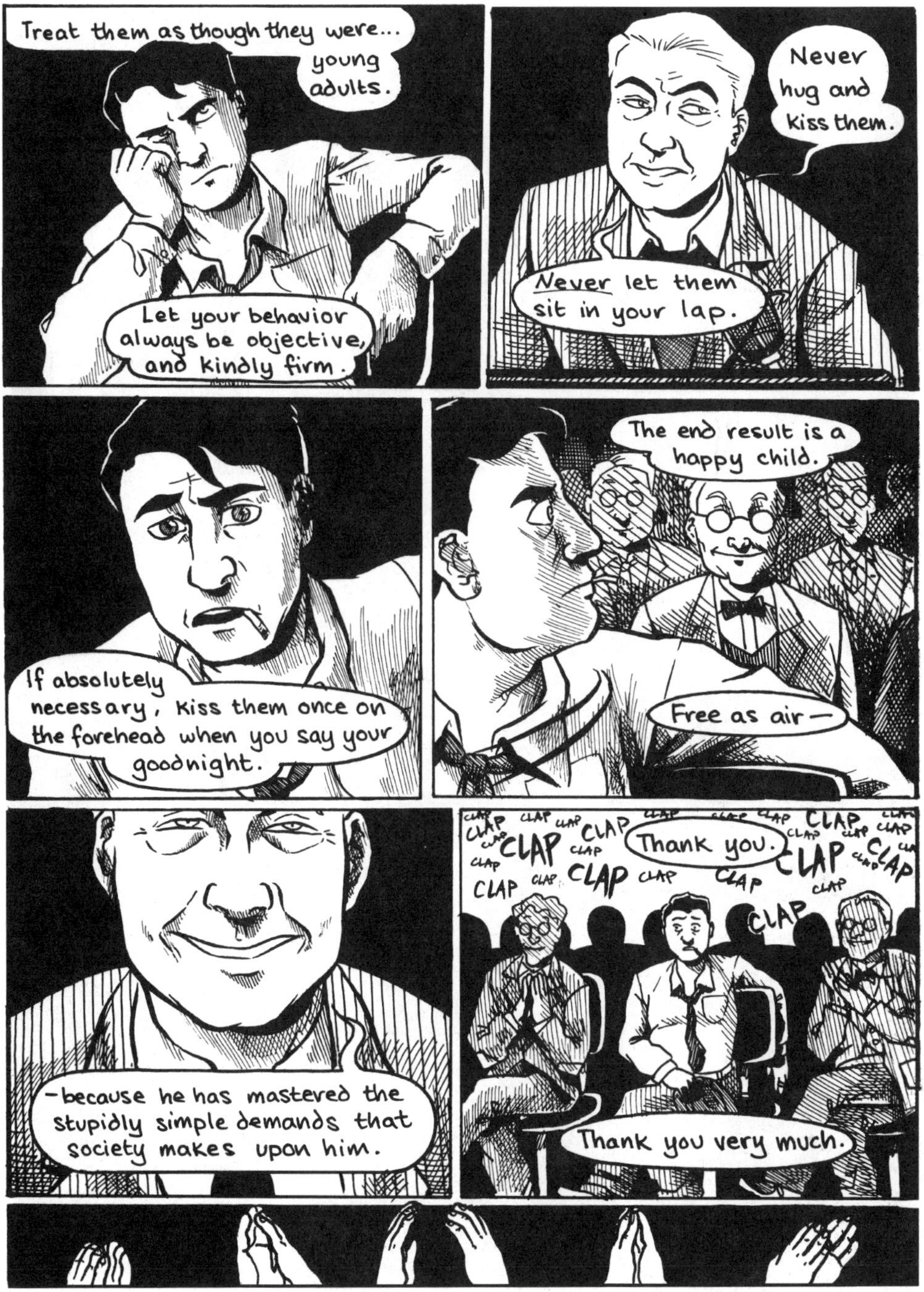
Treat them as though they were...
young adults.
Let your behavior always be objective, and kindly firm.
Never hug and kiss them.
Never let them sit in your lap.
If absolutely necessary, kiss them once on the forehead when you say your goodnight.
The end result is a happy child.
Free as air—
—because he has mastered the stupidly simple demands that society makes upon him.
CLAP CLAP CLAP CLAP
Thank you.
CLAP CLAP CLAP CLAP
Thank you very much.

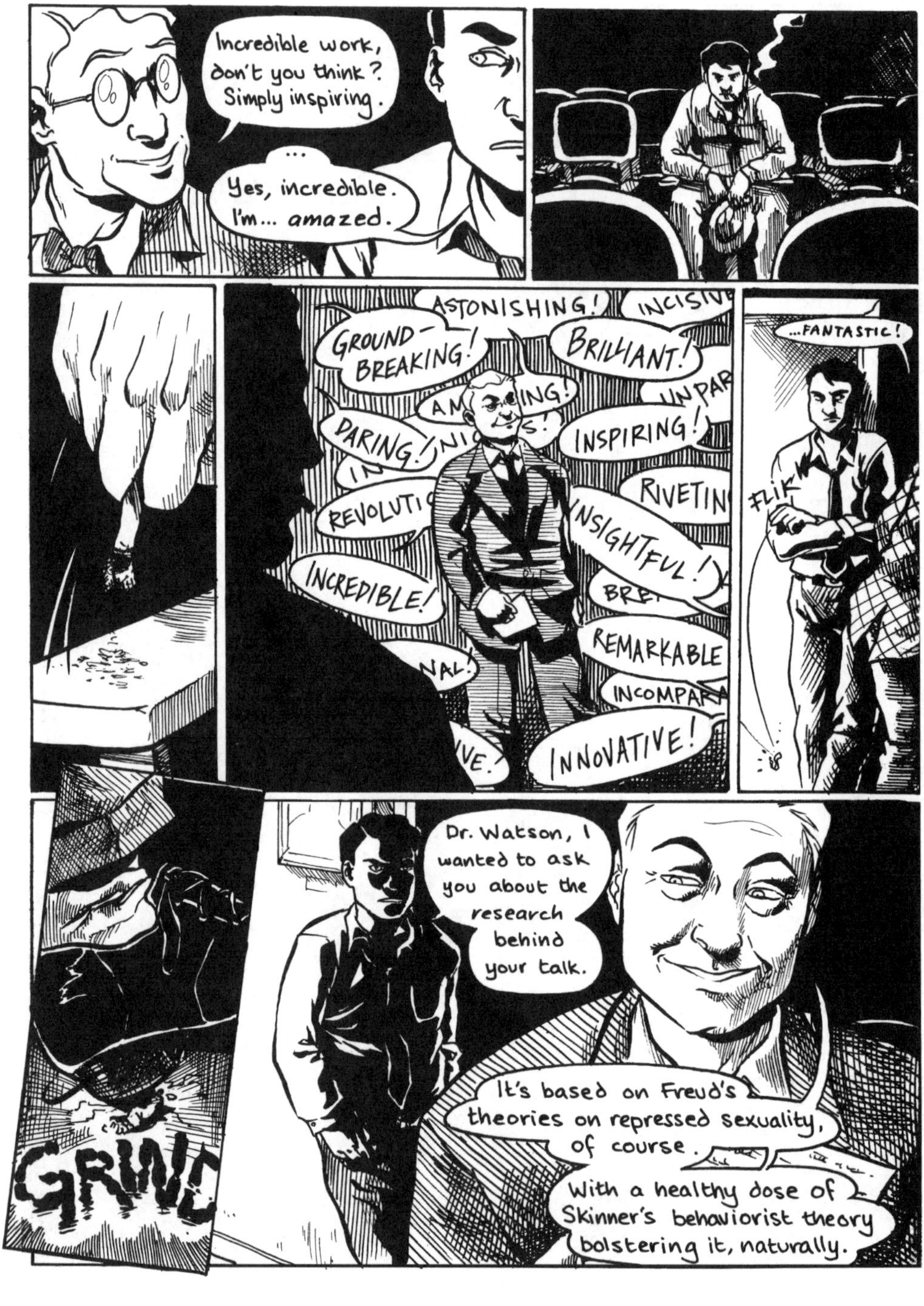
Incredible work, don't you think? Simply inspiring.
...
Yes, incredible. I'm... amazed.
ASTONISHING!
GROUND-BREAKING!
BRILLIANT!
DARING!
INSPIRING!
RIVETIN
REVOLUTI
INCREDIBLE!
INSIGHTFUL!
REMARKABLE
INCOMPAR
INNOVATIVE!
...FANTASTIC!
FLIK
GRIND
Dr. Watson, I wanted to ask you about the research behind your talk.
It's based on Freud's theories on repressed sexuality, of course.
With a healthy dose of Skinner's behaviorist theory bolstering it, naturally.

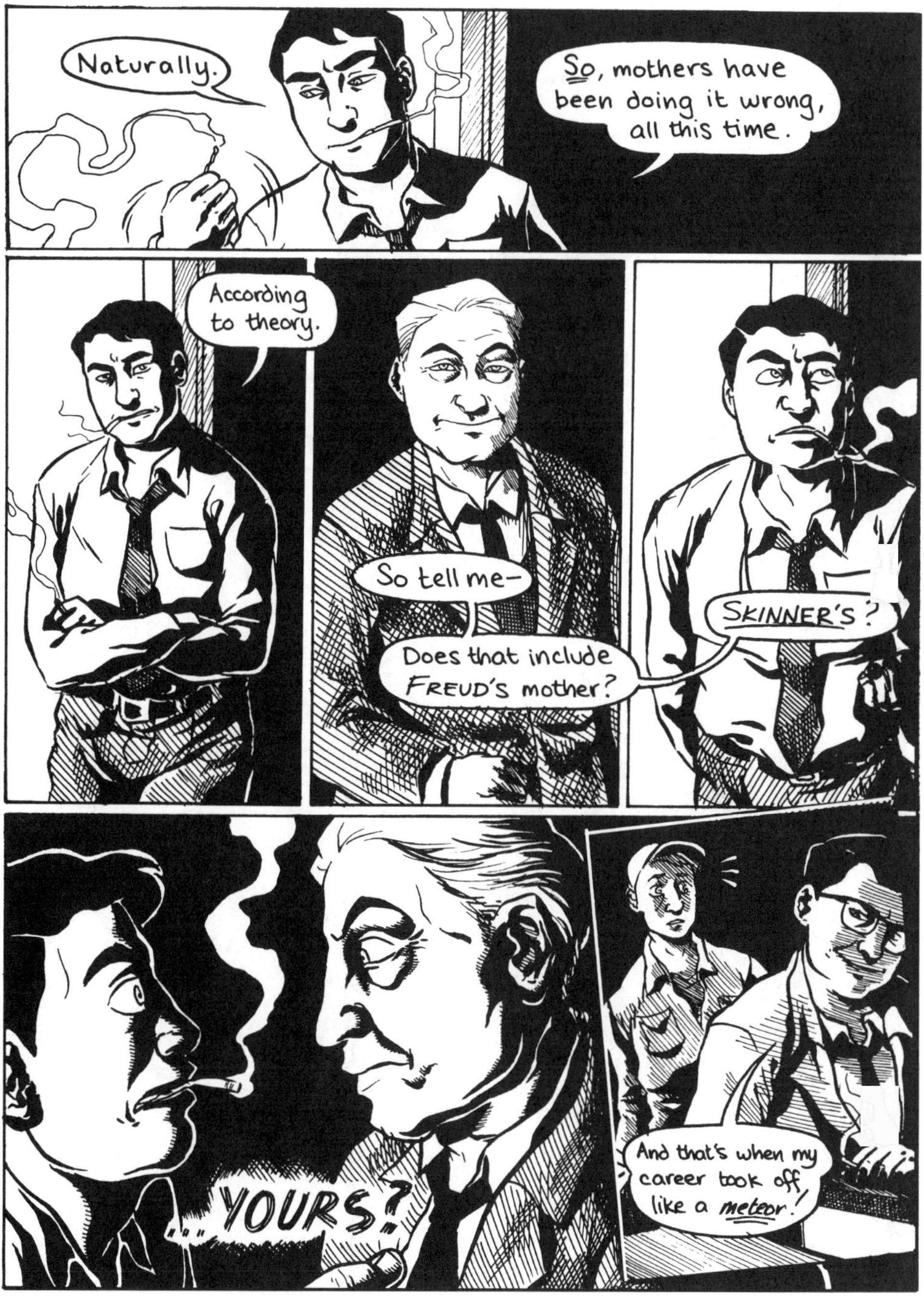
Naturally.
So, mothers have been doing it wrong, all this time.
According to theory.
So tell me-
Does that include FREUD'S mother?
SKINNER'S?
..."YOURS?"
And that's when my career took off like a meteor!

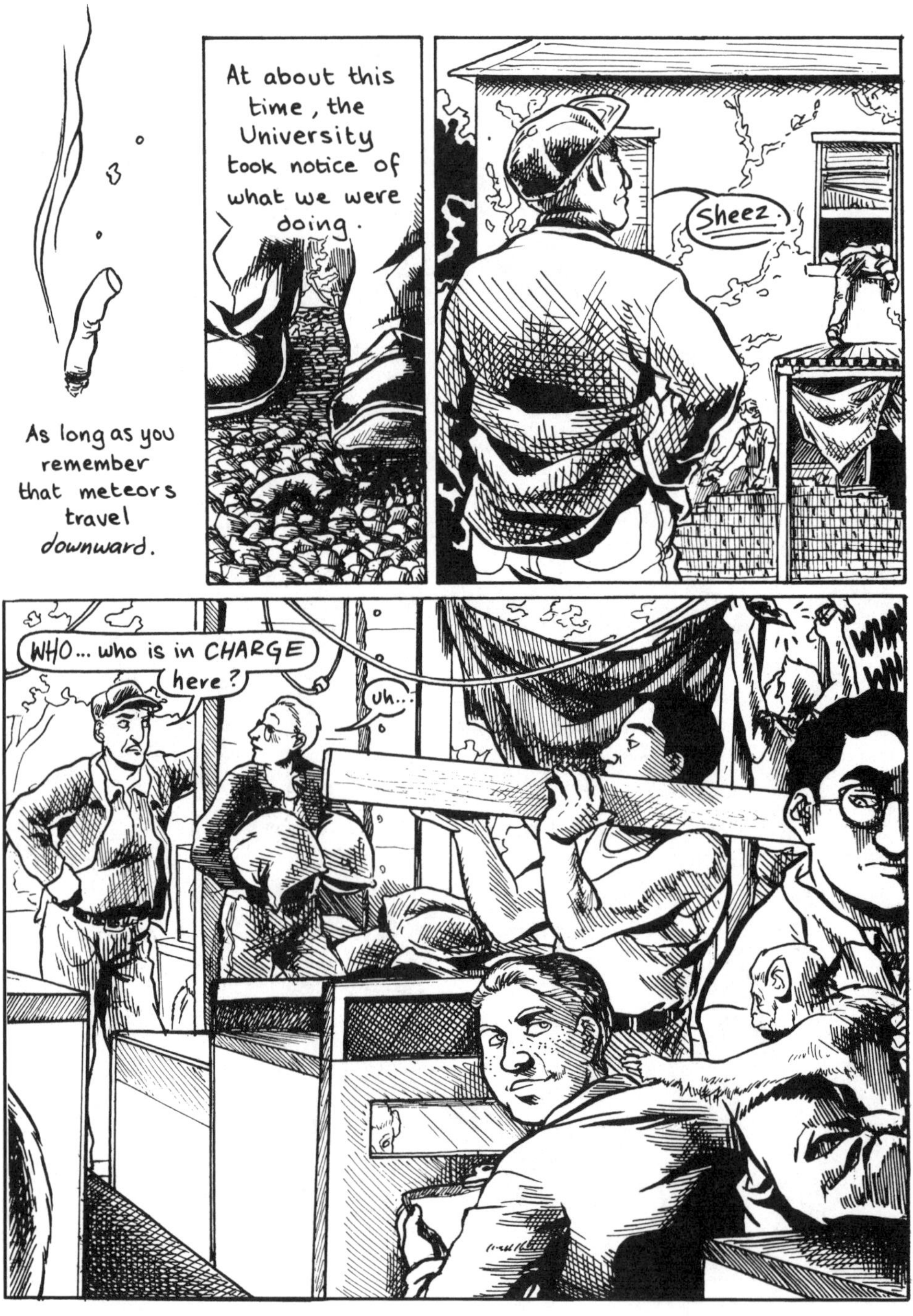
As long as you remember that meteors travel *downward*.
At about this time, the University took notice of what we were doing.
Sheez.
WHO... who is in CHARGE here?
uh...

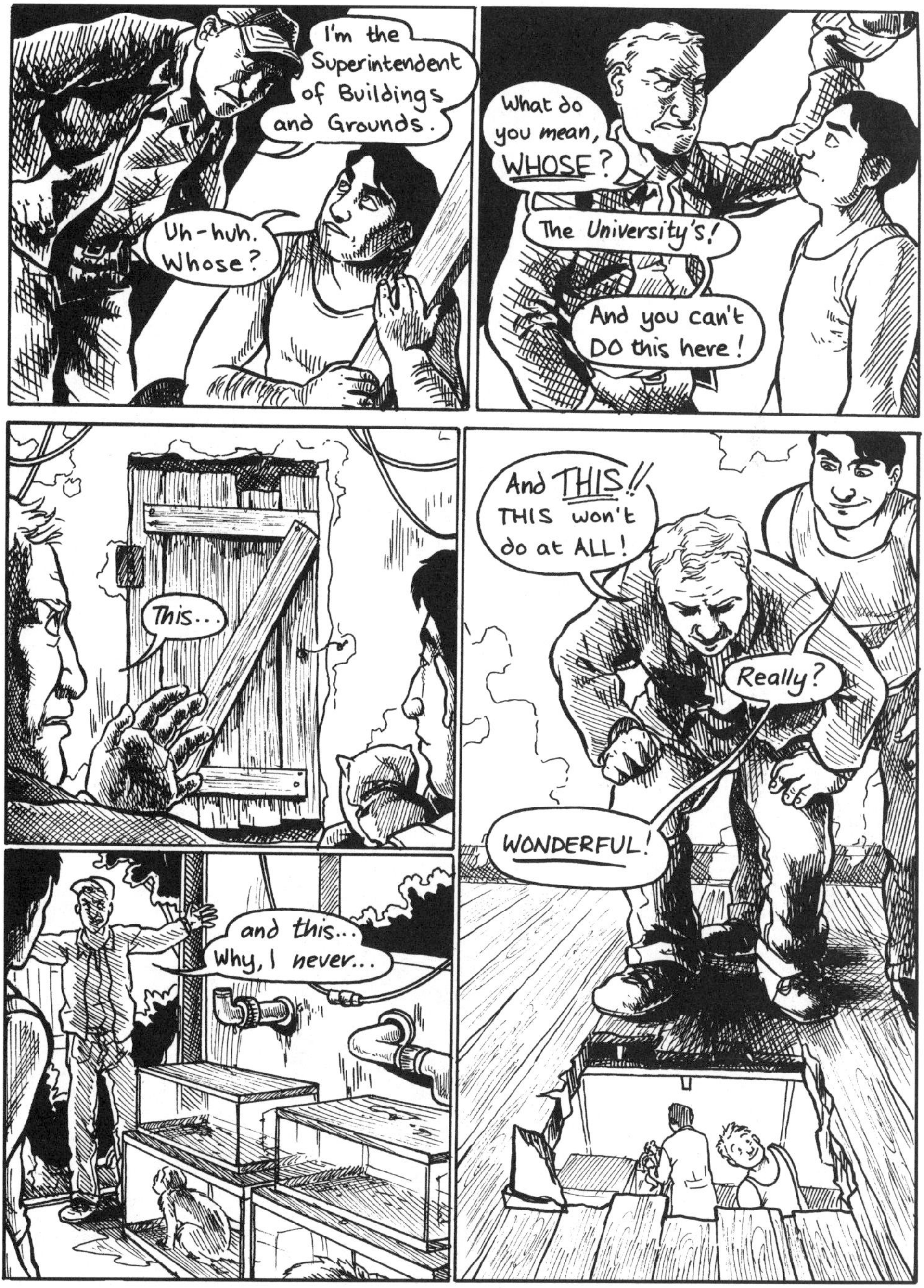
I'm the Superintendent of Buildings and Grounds.
Uh-huh. Whose?
What do you mean, WHOSE?
The University's!
And you can't DO this here!
This...
and this... Why, I never...
And THIS!! THIS won't do at ALL!
Really?
WONDERFUL!

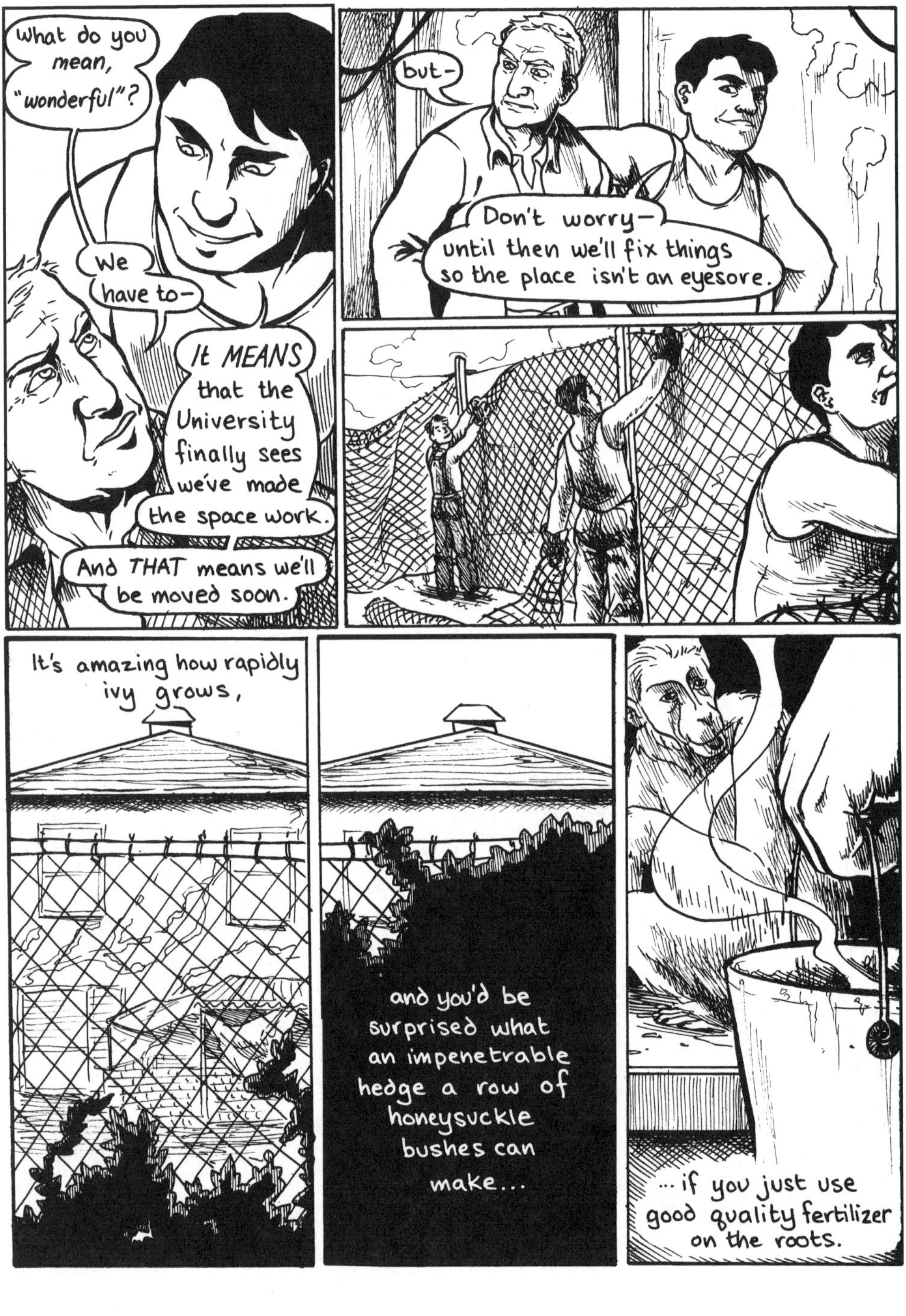
What do you mean, "wonderful"?
We have to-
It MEANS that the University finally sees we've made the space work.
And THAT means we'll be moved soon.
but-
Don't worry- until then we'll fix things so the place isn't an eyesore.
It's amazing how rapidly ivy grows,
and you'd be surprised what an impenetrable hedge a row of honeysuckle bushes can make...
...if you just use good quality fertilizer on the roots.

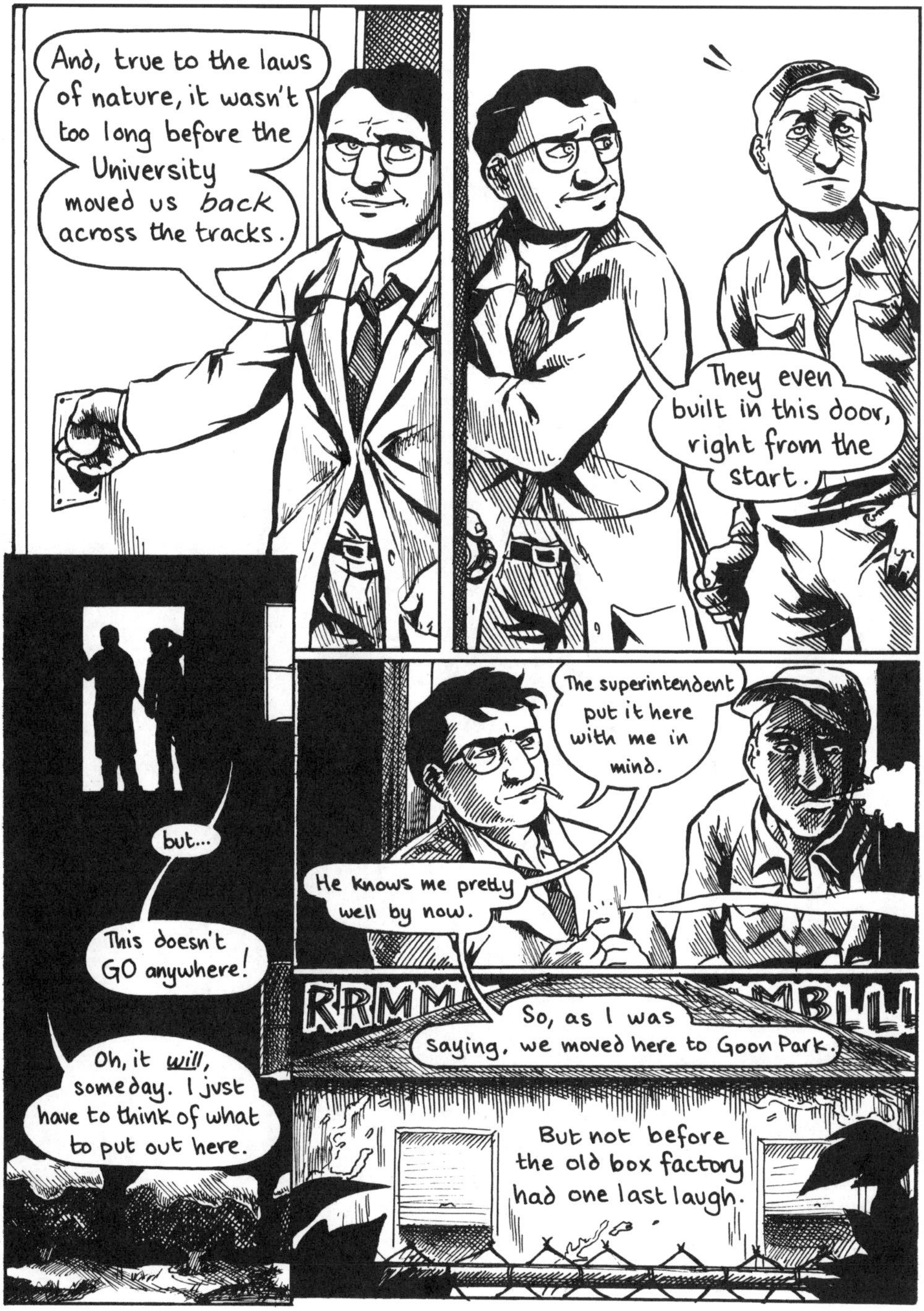
And, true to the laws of nature, it wasn't too long before the University moved us *back* across the tracks.
They even built in this door, right from the start.
The superintendent put it here with me in mind.
He knows me pretty well by now.
...
but...
This doesn't GO anywhere!
Oh, it *will*, someday. I just have to think of what to put out here.
So, as I was saying, we moved here to Goon Park.
But not before the old box factory had one last laugh.

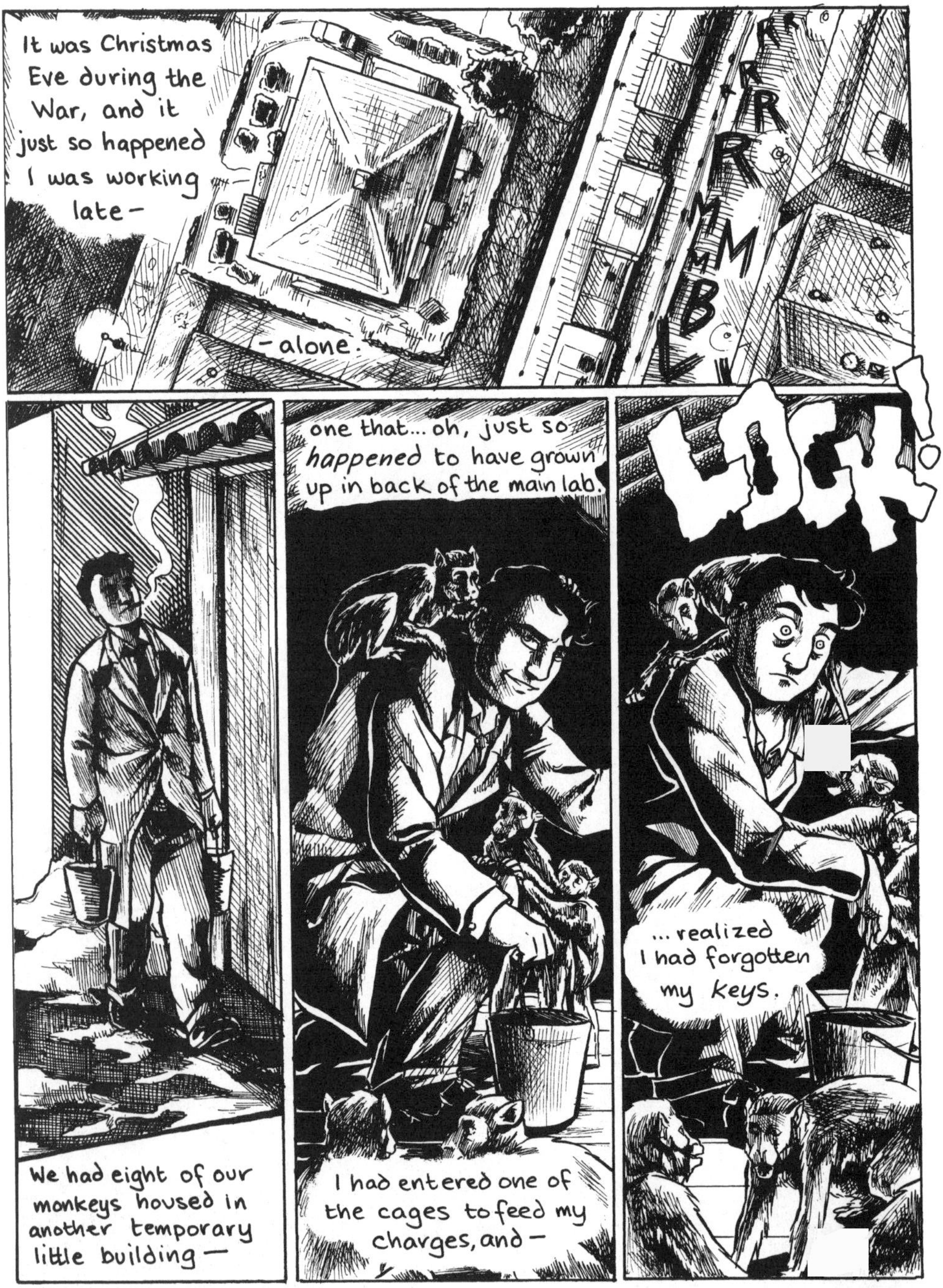

It was Christmas Eve during the War, and it just so happened I was working late –
– alone.
RRRRMMMBL
We had eight of our monkeys housed in another temporary little building —
one that... oh, just so *happened* to have grown up in back of the main lab.
I had entered one of the cages to feed my charges, and –
LOCK!
... realized I had forgotten my keys.

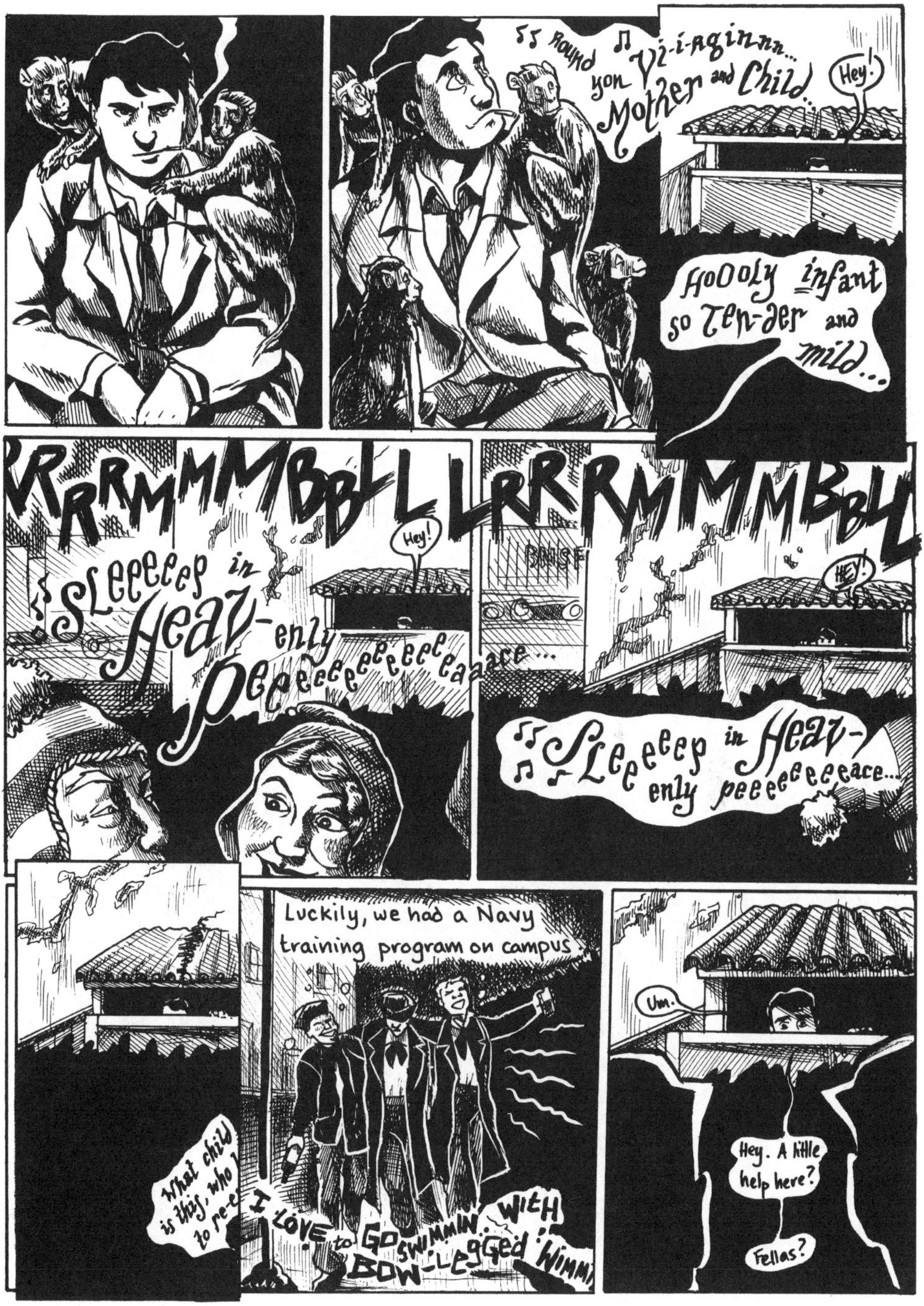
♫♫ Round yon Vi-i-irginnn... Mother and Child...
Hey!
HoOoly infant so ten-der and mild...
RRRMMMBBLL
Hey!
Sleeeeep in Heav-enly peeeeeeeeeeeaaace...
LRRRMMMBBL
BRISE
HEY!
♫♫ Sleeeeep in Heav-enly peeeeeeeeace...
What child is this, who to re-e
Luckily, we had a Navy training program on campus.
I LOVE to GO SWIMMIN WITH BOW-LEgged WIMMI
Um.
Hey. A little help here?
Fellas?

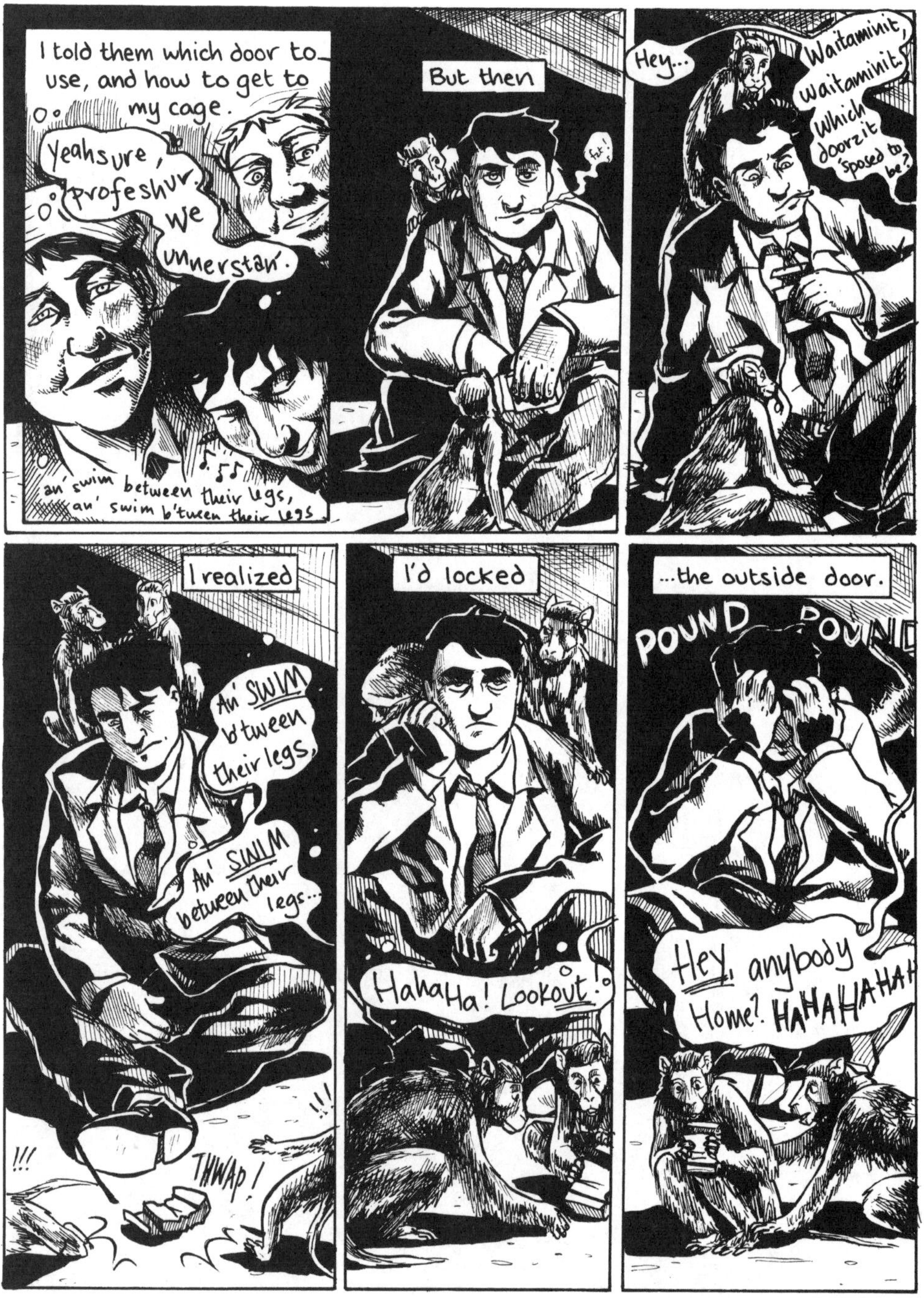
I told them which door to use, and how to get to my cage.
Yeahsure, profeshur. We unnerstan'.
an' swim between their legs, an' swim b'tween their legs
But then
fft!
Hey...
Waitaminit, waitaminit. Which doorz it 'sposed to be?
I realized
An' SWIM b'tween their legs.
An' SWIM between their legs...
!!!
THWAP!
!!!
I'd locked
HahaHa! Lookout!
...the outside door.
POUND POUND
Hey, anybody Home? HAHAHAHAH

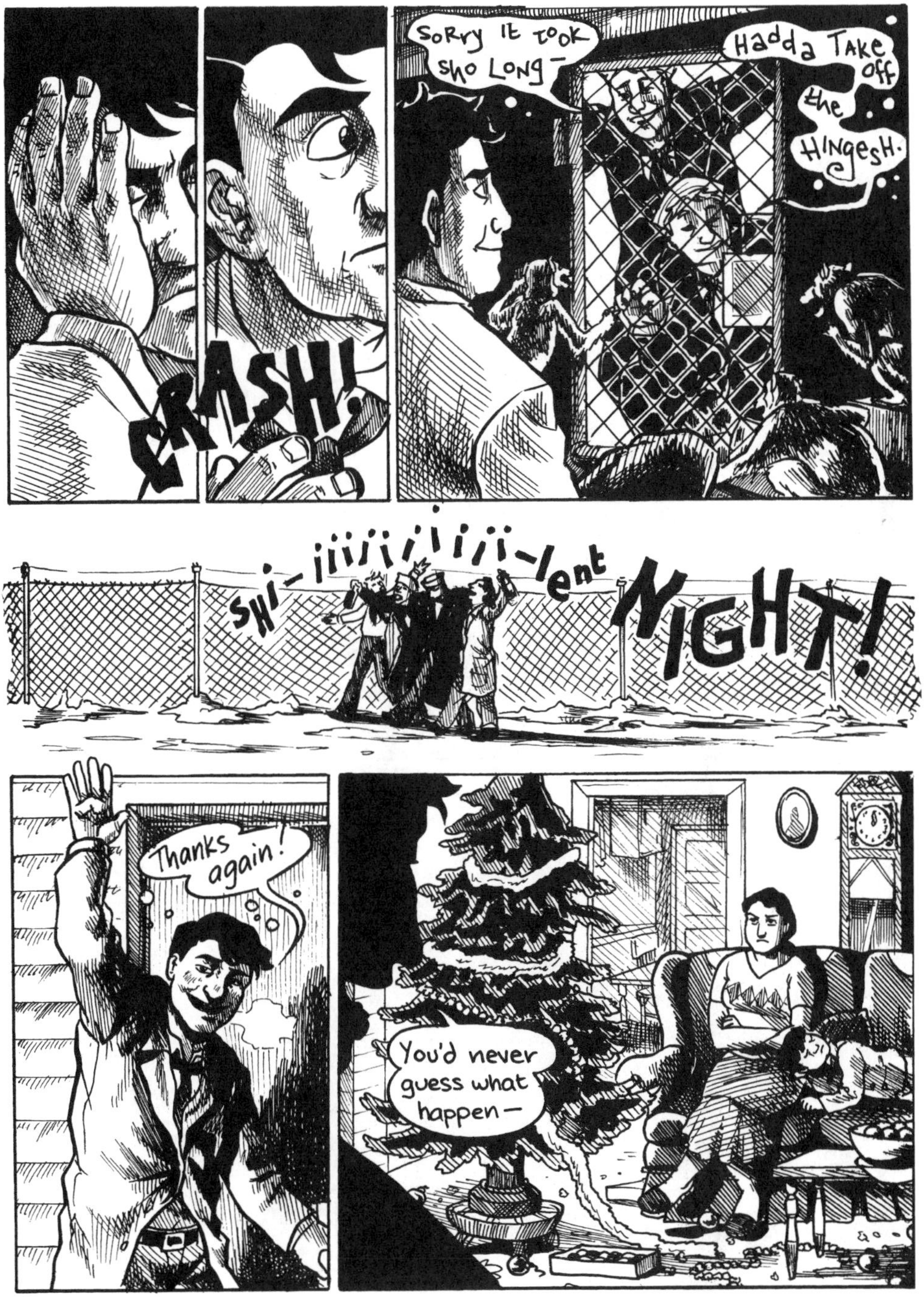
CRASH!
Sorry it took sho long—
Hadda take off the hingesh.
Shi—iiiiiiii—lent NIGHT!
Thanks again!
You'd never guess what happen—

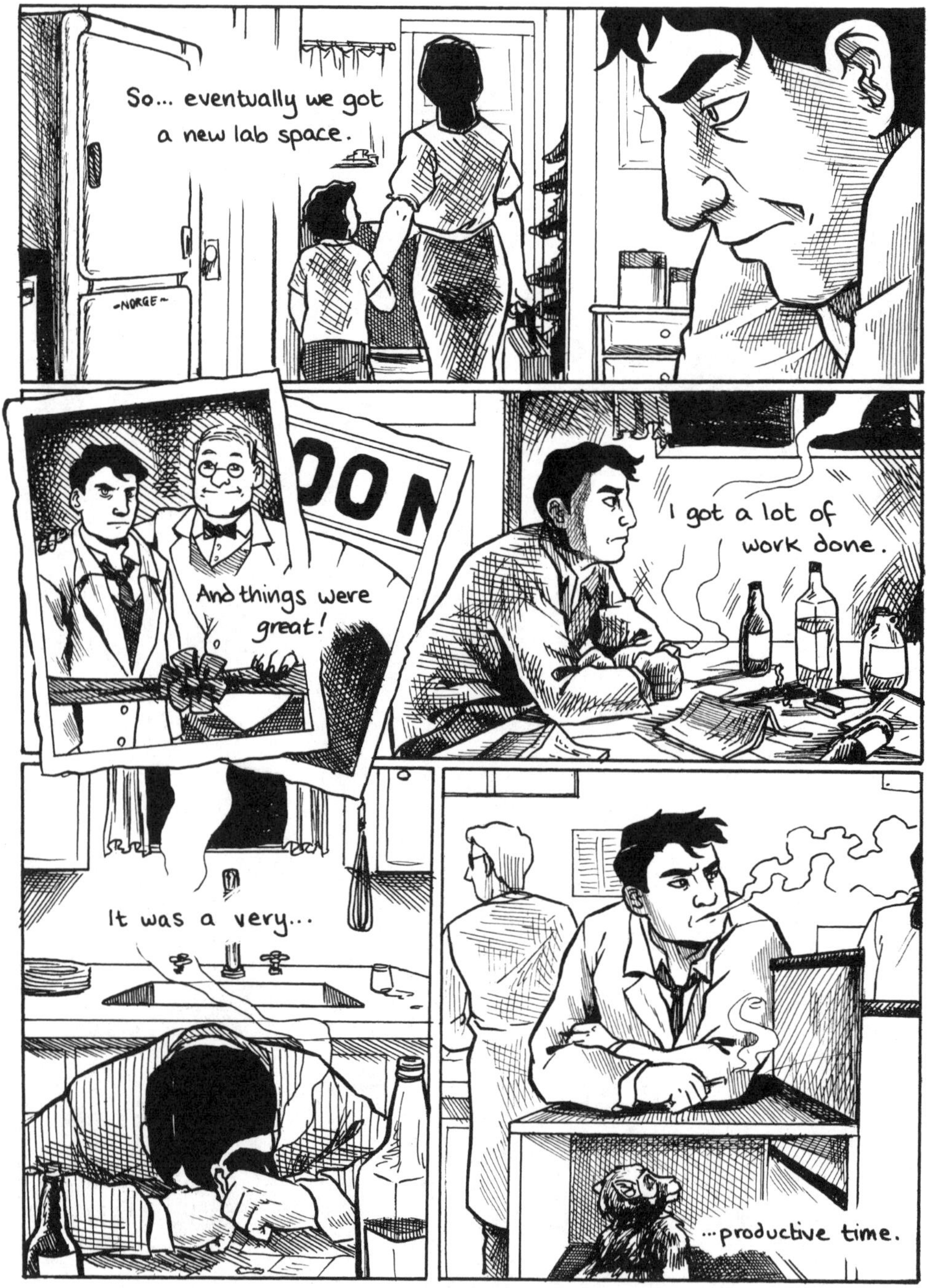
So... eventually we got a new lab space.
-NORGE-
And things were great!
I got a lot of work done.
It was a very...
...productive time.

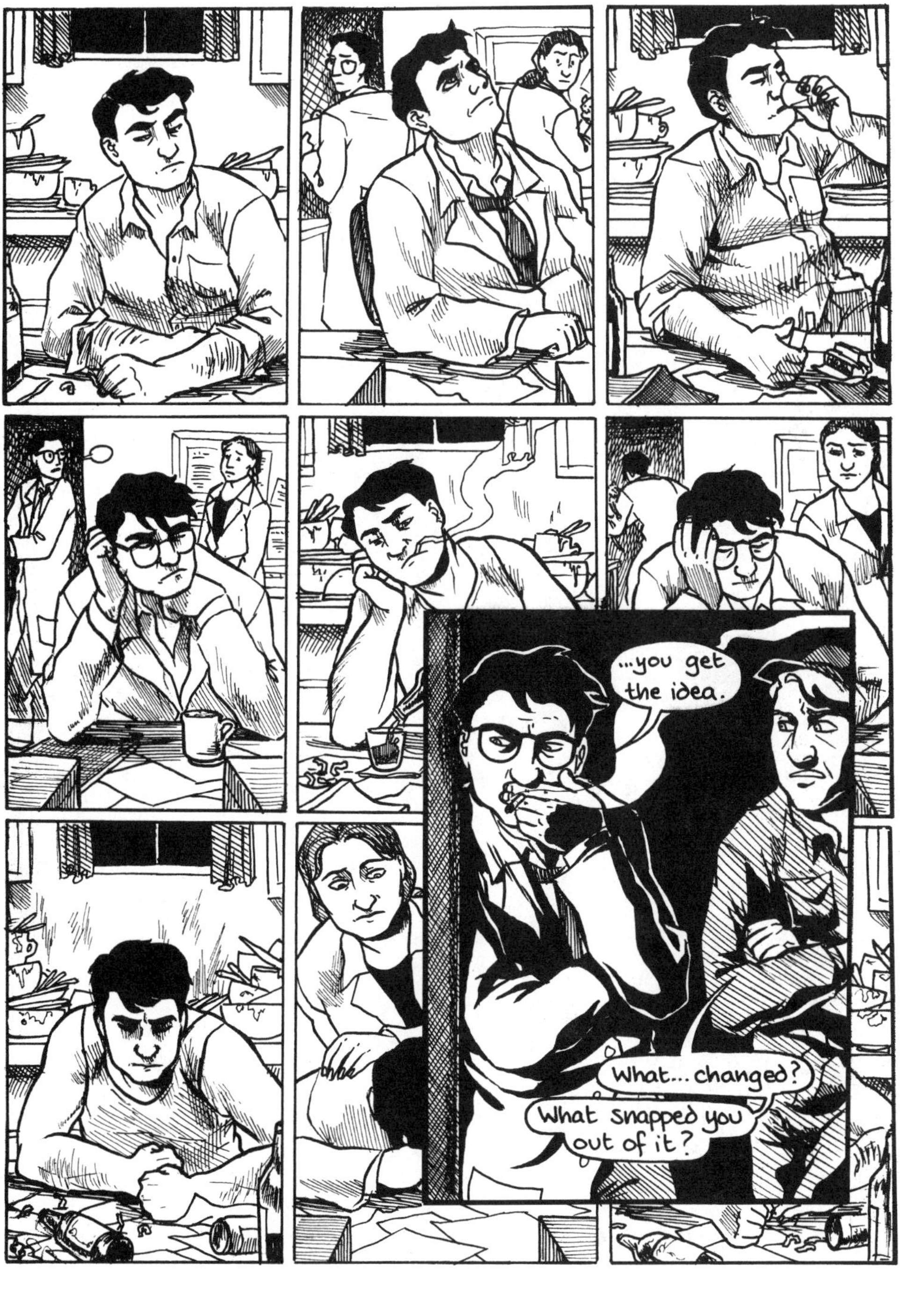
...you get the idea.
What... changed?
What snapped you out of it?

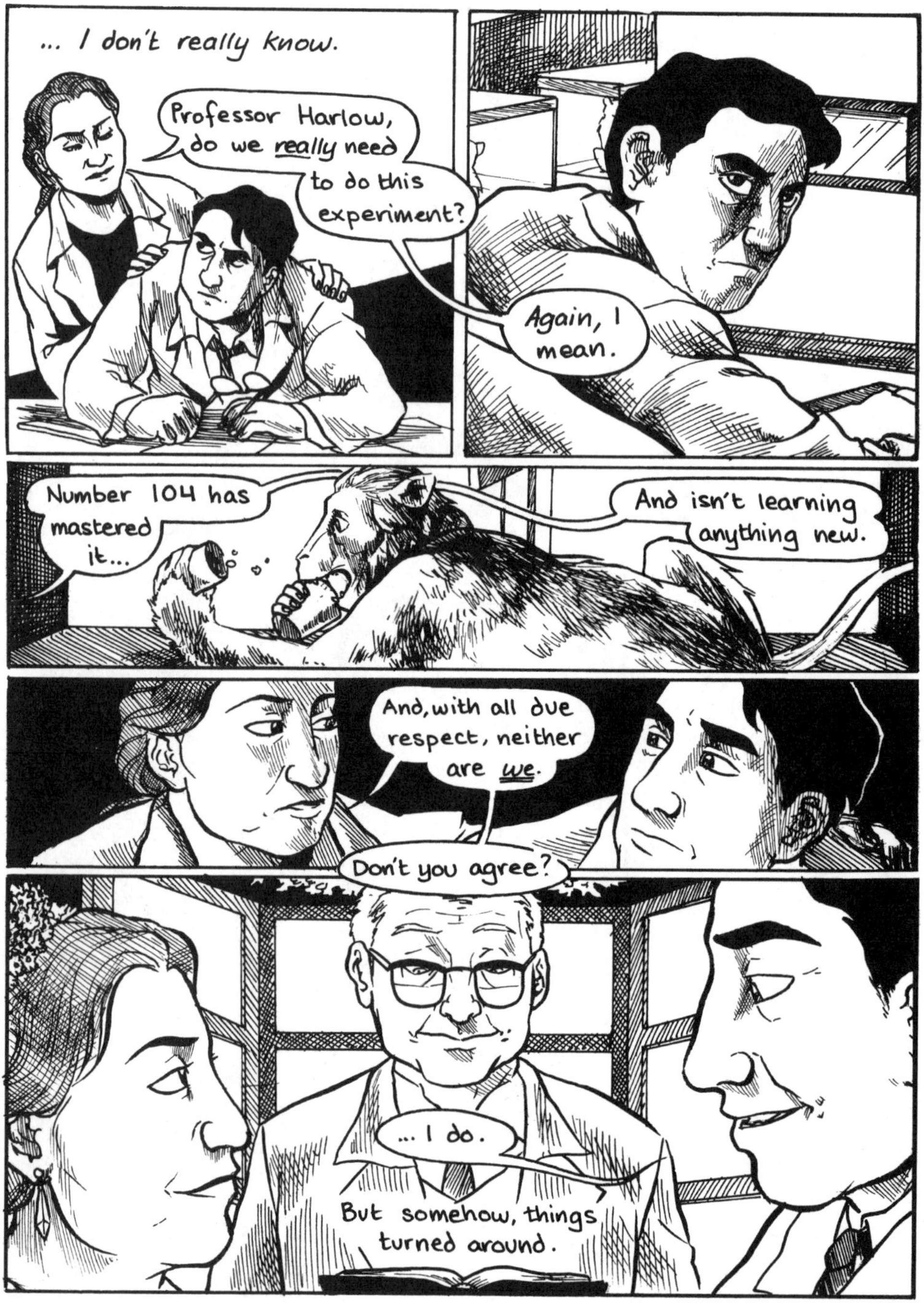
... I don't really know.
Professor Harlow, do we really need to do this experiment?
Again, I mean.
Number 104 has mastered it...
And isn't learning anything new.
And, with all due respect, neither are we.
Don't you agree?
... I do.
But somehow, things turned around.

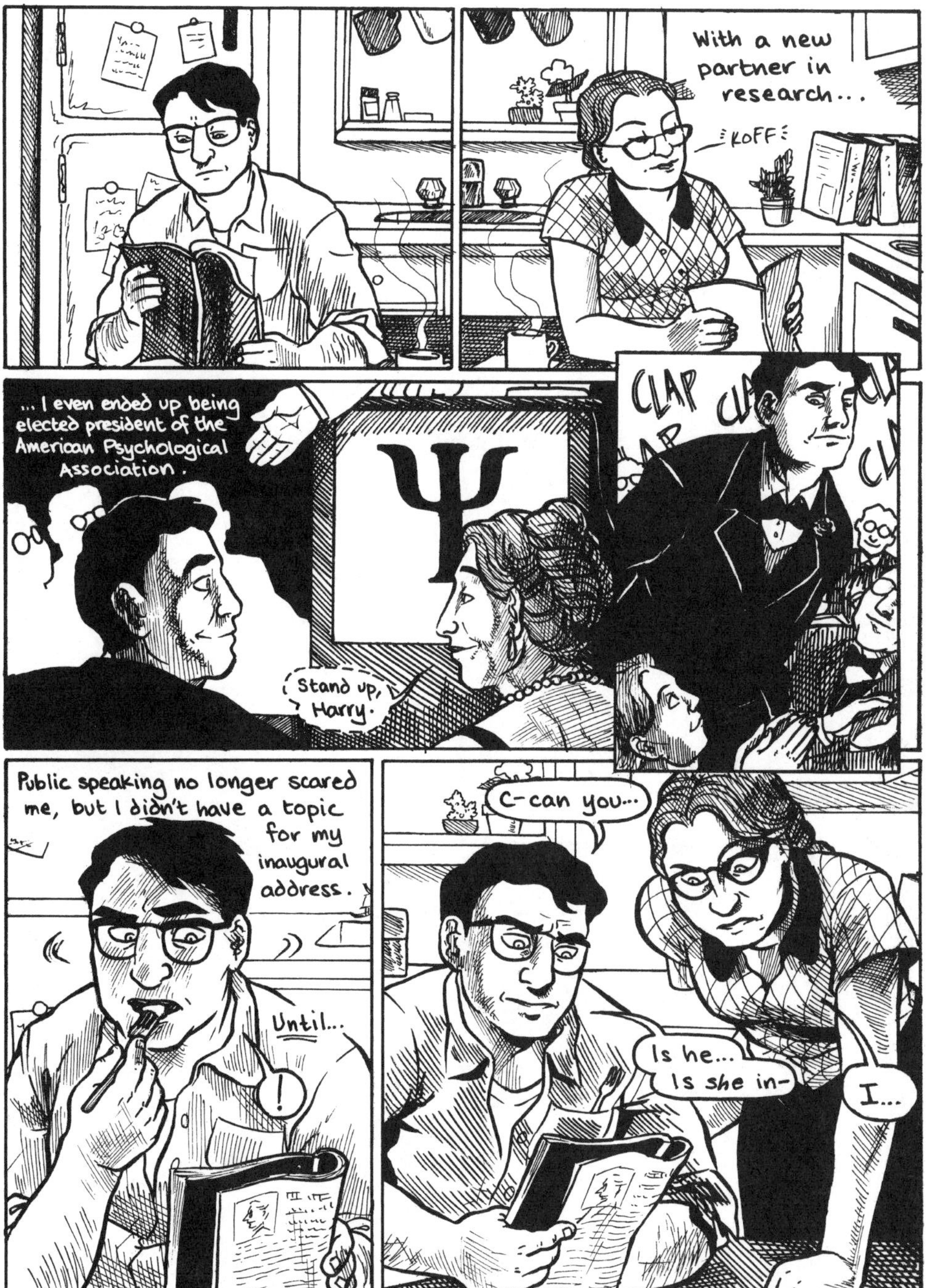
With a new partner in research...
KOFF
... I even ended up being elected president of the American Psychological Association.
Ψ
Stand up, Harry.
CLAP
CLAP
CLAP
CLAP
CLAP
Public speaking no longer scared me, but I didn't have a topic for my inaugural address.
Until...
!
C-can you...
Is he... Is she in-
I...

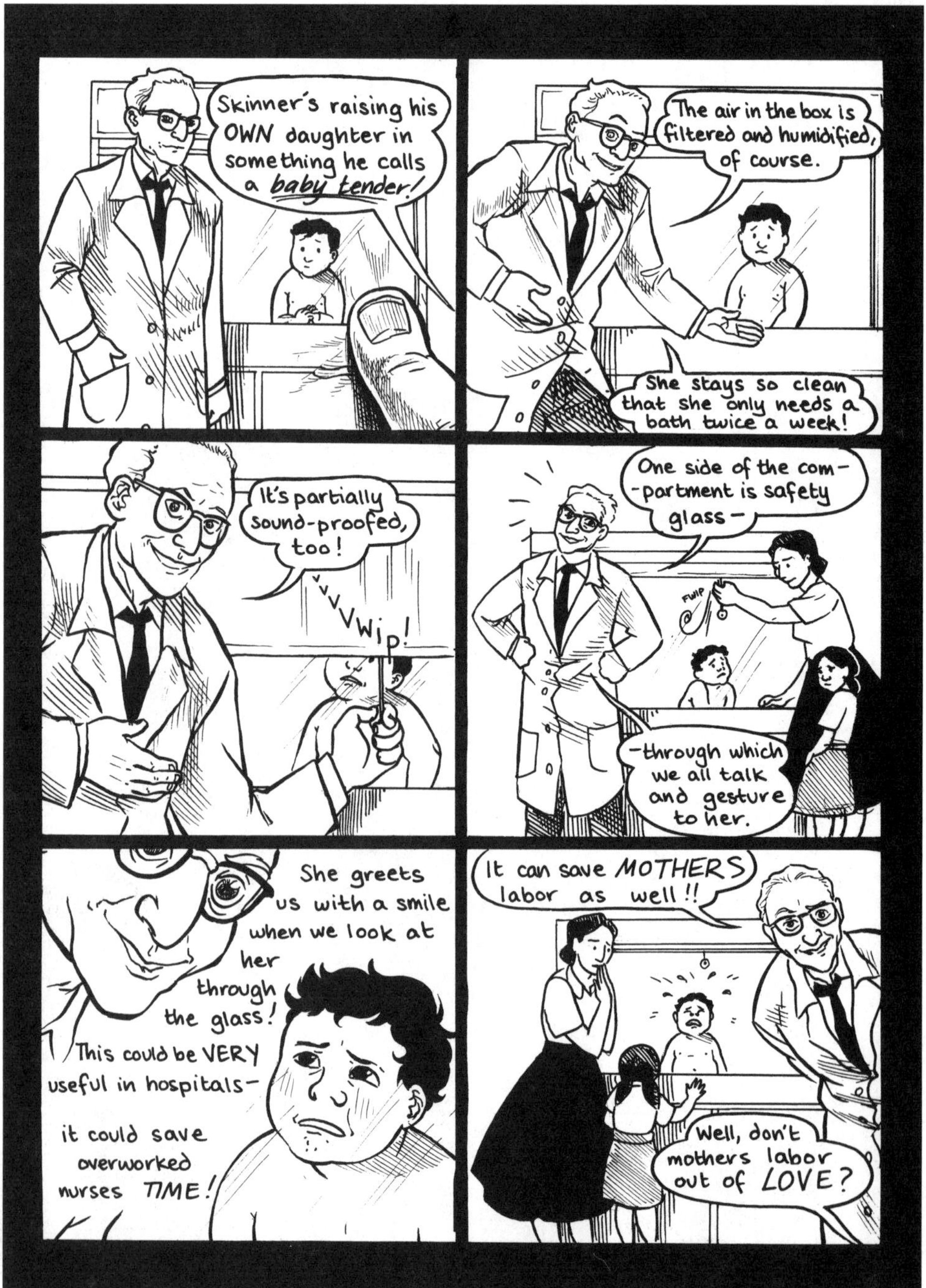
Skinner's raising his OWN daughter in something he calls a baby tender!
The air in the box is filtered and humidified, of course.
She stays so clean that she only needs a bath twice a week!
It's partially sound-proofed, too!
vvvvWip!
One side of the com- -partment is safety glass-
FWIP
-through which we all talk and gesture to her.
She greets us with a smile when we look at her through the glass!
This could be VERY useful in hospitals-
it could save overworked nurses TIME!
It can save MOTHERS labor as well!!
Well, don't mothers labor out of LOVE?

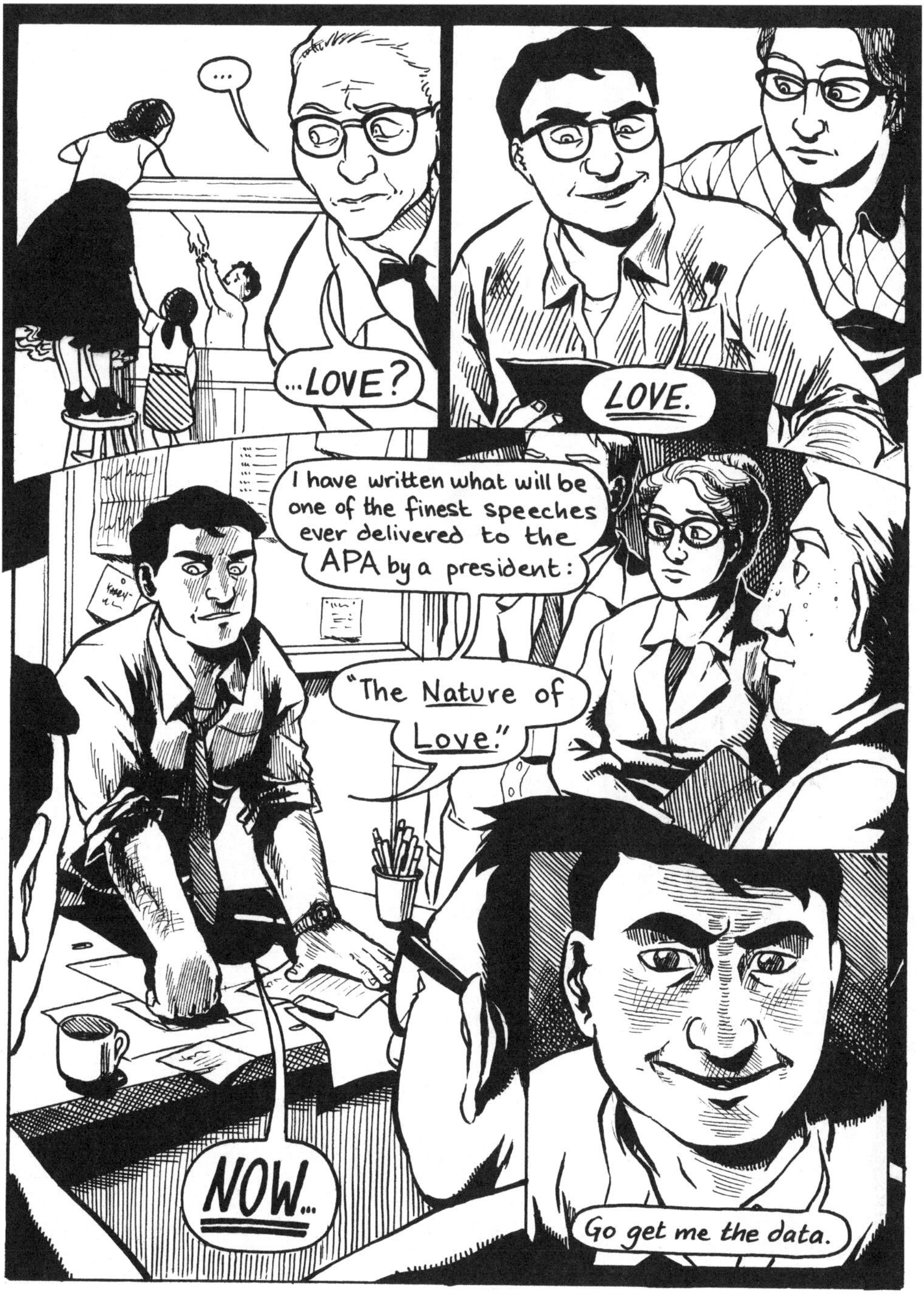
...
...LOVE?
LOVE.
I have written what will be one of the finest speeches ever delivered to the APA by a president:
"The Nature of Love."
NOW...
Go get me the data.

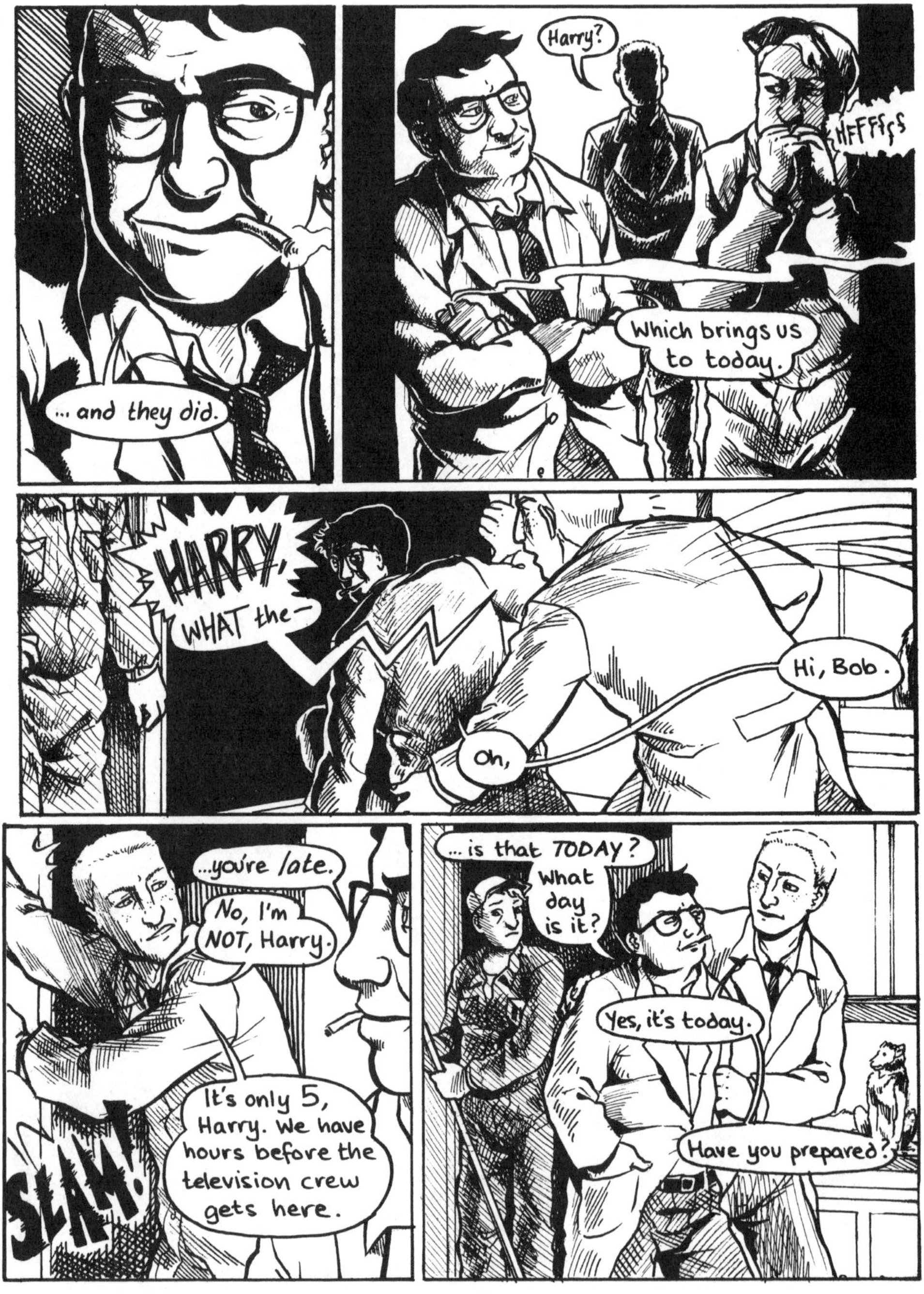
... and they did.
Harry?
HFFFfſs
Which brings us to today.
HARRY, WHAT the—
Oh,
Hi, Bob.
...you're late.
No, I'm NOT, Harry.
It's only 5, Harry. We have hours before the television crew gets here.
SLAM!
... is that TODAY?
What day is it?
Yes, it's today.
Have you prepared?

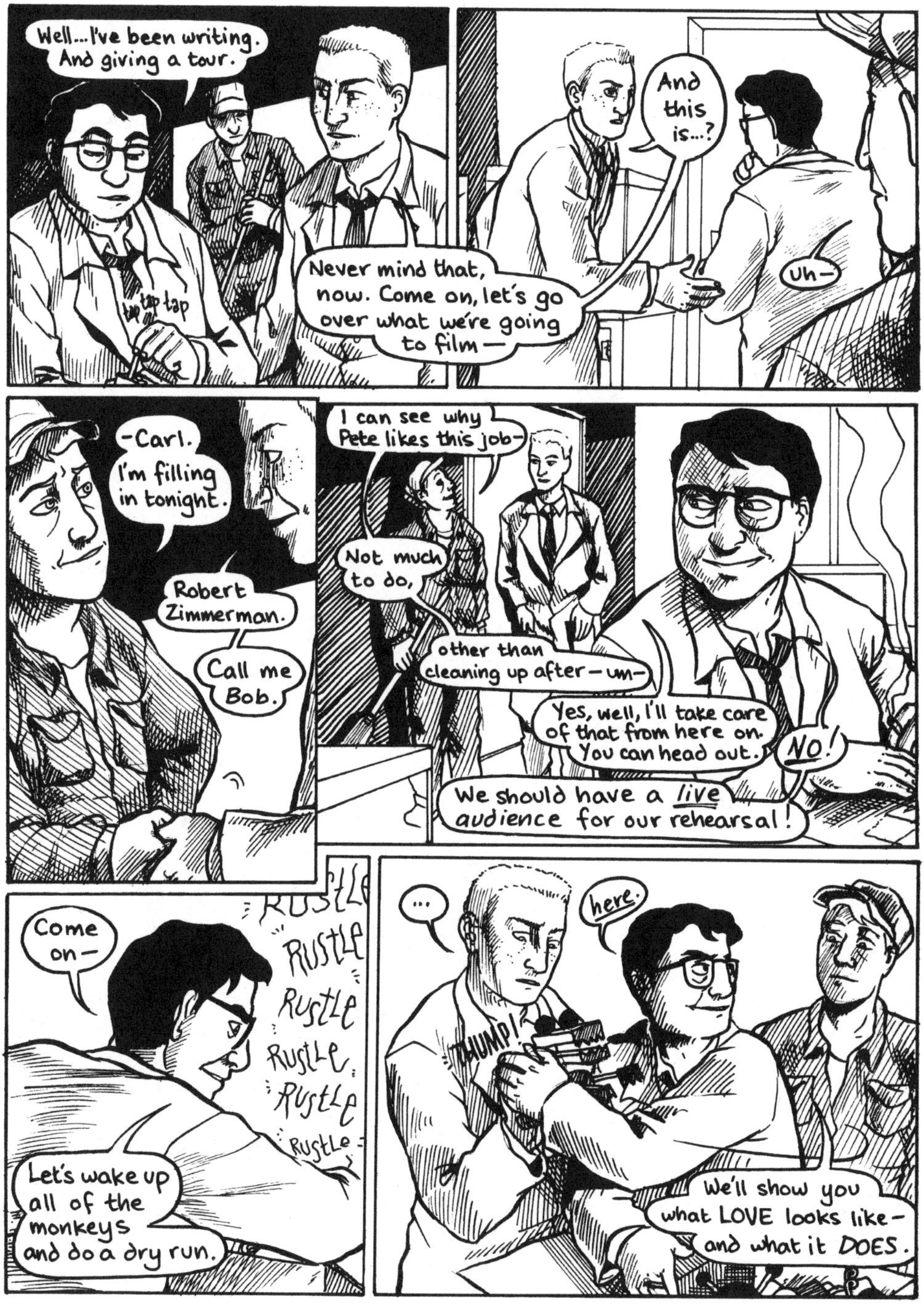
Well...I've been writing. And giving a tour.
tap tap tap
Never mind that, now. Come on, let's go over what we're going to film—
And this is...?
Uh—
-Carl. I'm filling in tonight.
Robert Zimmerman.
Call me Bob.
I can see why Pete likes this job—
Not much to do,
other than cleaning up after—um—
Yes, well, I'll take care of that from here on. You can head out.
No!
We should have a live audience for our rehearsal!
Come on—
RUSTLE
RUSTLE
RUSTLE
RUSTLE
RUSTLE
RUSTLE
Let's wake up all of the monkeys and do a dry run.
...
here.
THUMP!
We'll show you what LOVE looks like— and what it DOES.

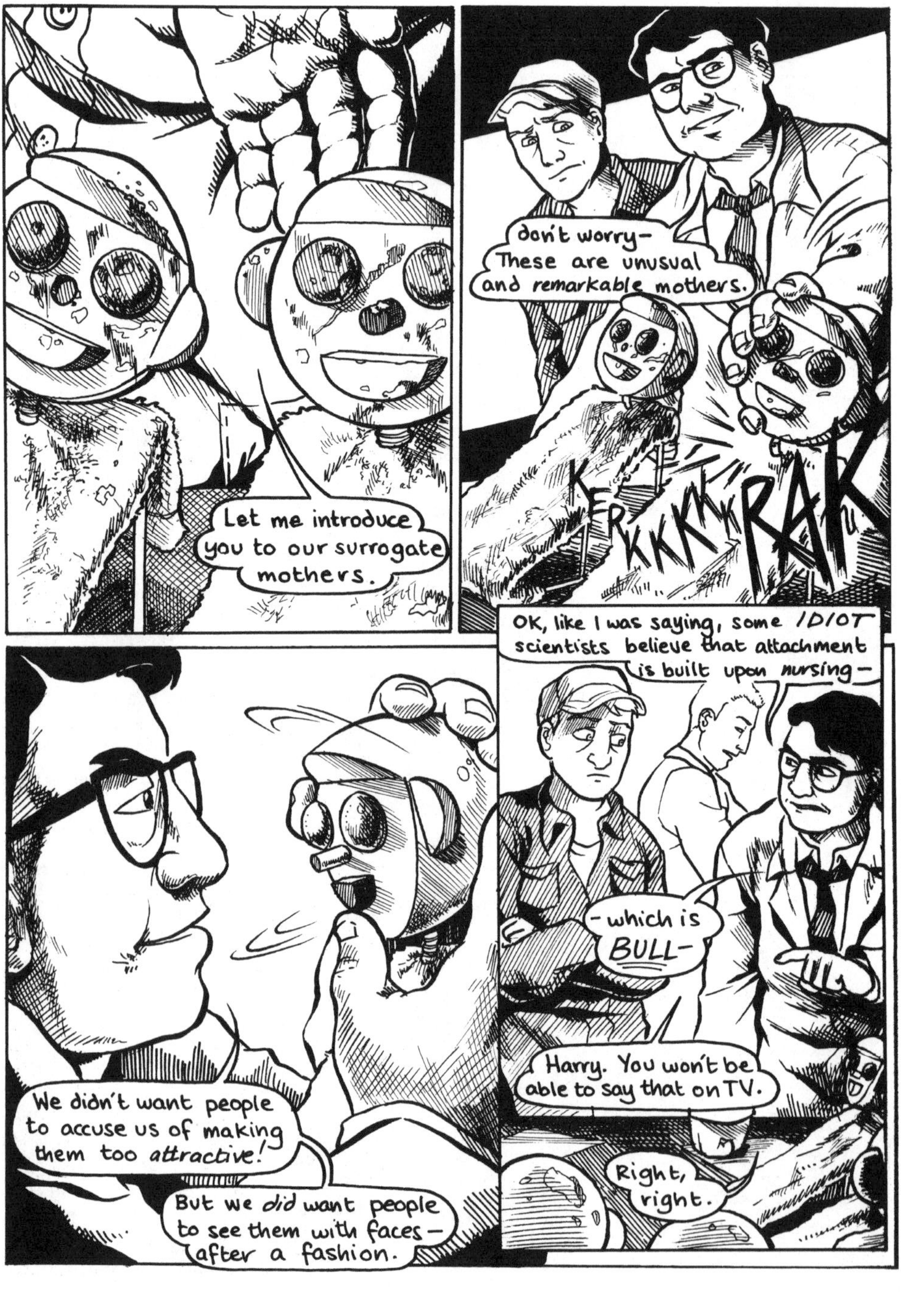
Let me introduce you to our surrogate mothers.
don't worry- These are unusual and remarkable mothers.
KERKKKKKRAK
We didn't want people to accuse us of making them too attractive!
But we did want people to see them with faces- after a fashion.
OK, like I was saying, some IDIOT scientists believe that attachment is built upon nursing-
-which is BULL-
Harry. You won't be able to say that on TV.
Right, right.

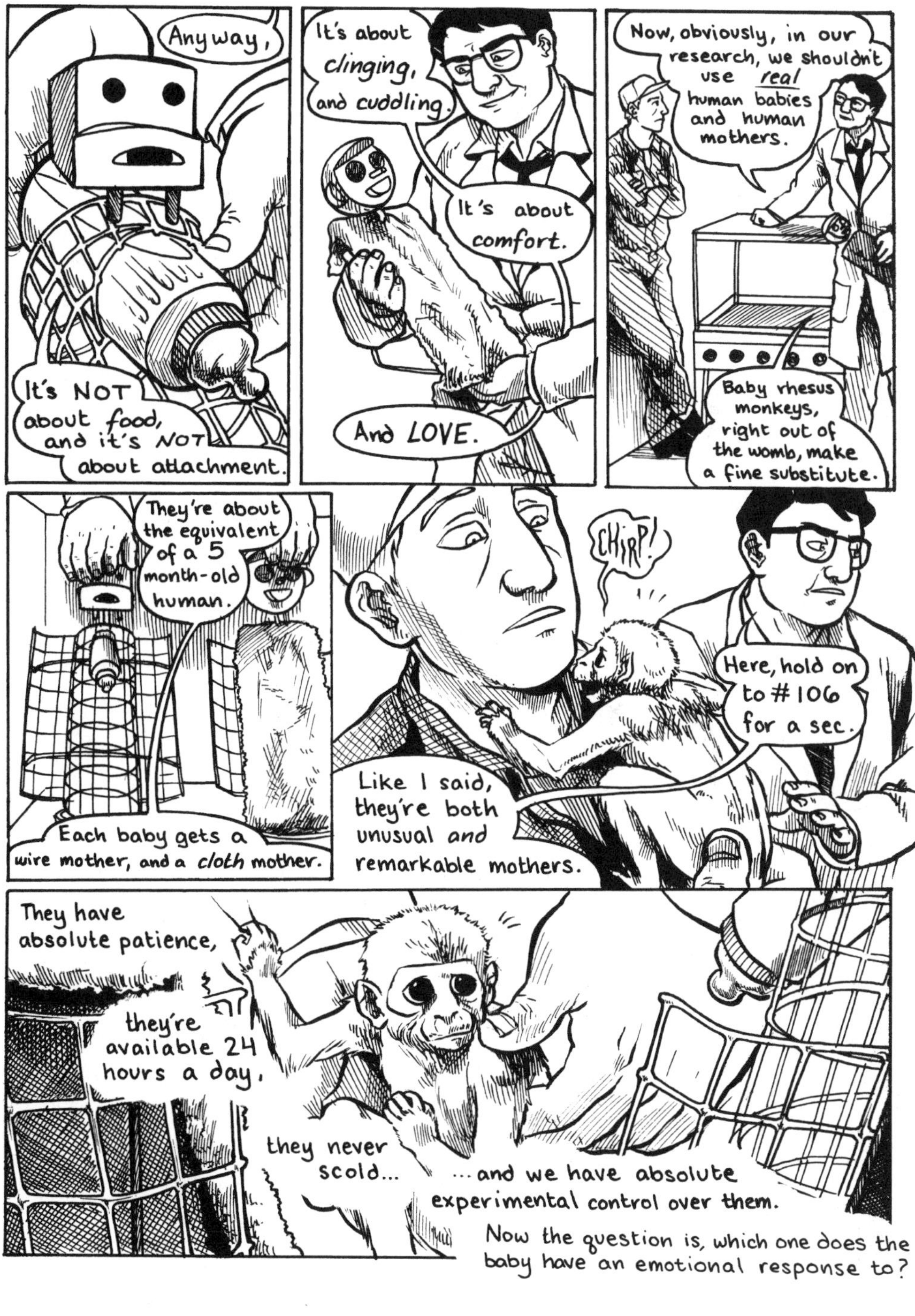
Anyway,
It's NOT about food, and it's NOT about attachment.
It's about clinging, and cuddling.
It's about comfort.
And LOVE.
Now, obviously, in our research, we shouldn't use real human babies and human mothers.
Baby rhesus monkeys, right out of the womb, make a fine substitute.
They're about the equivalent of a 5 month-old human.
Each baby gets a wire mother, and a cloth mother.
CHIRP!
Here, hold on to #106 for a sec.
Like I said, they're both unusual and remarkable mothers.
They have absolute patience,
they're available 24 hours a day,
they never scold...
...and we have absolute experimental control over them.
Now the question is, which one does the baby have an emotional response to?

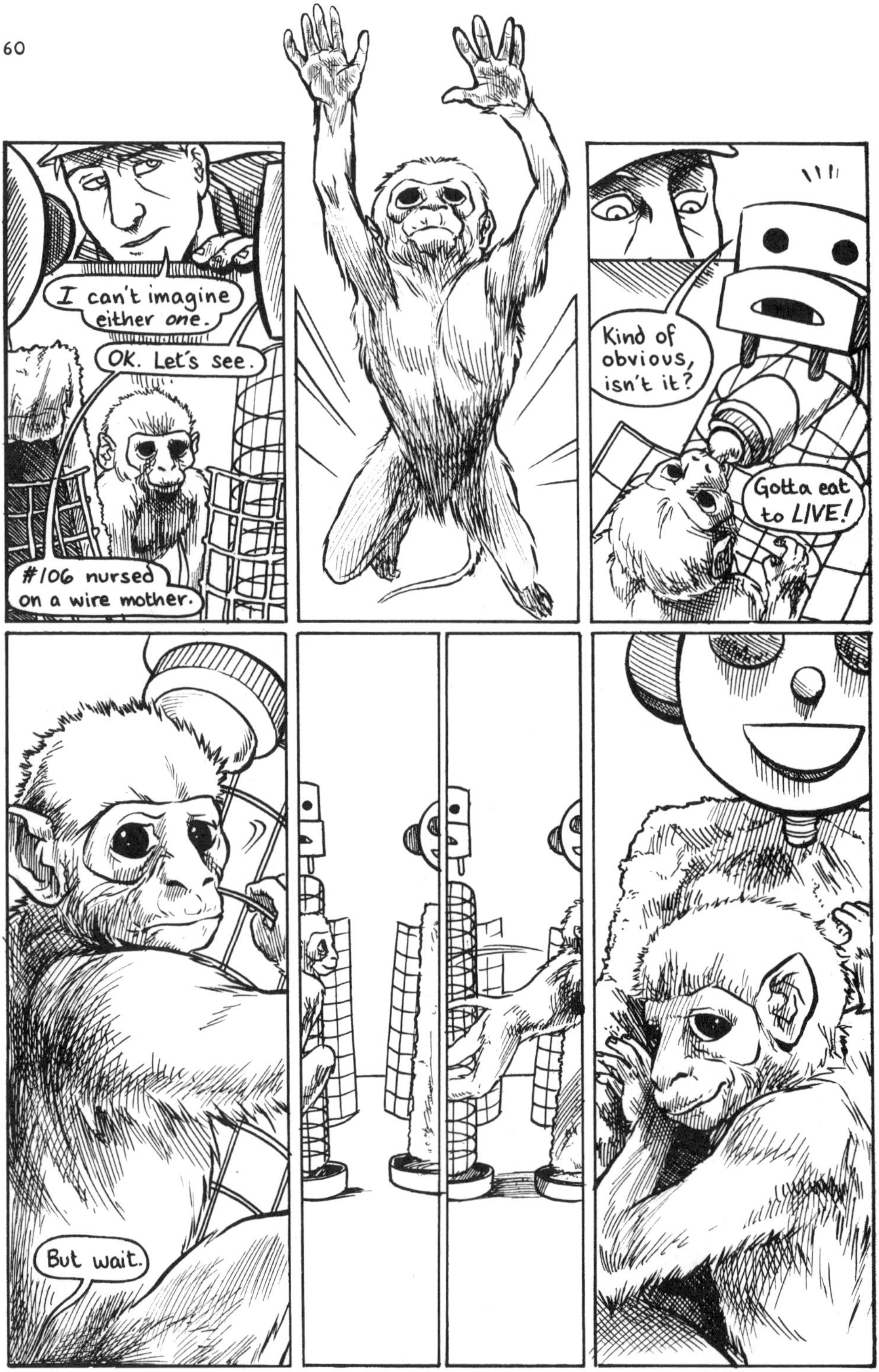
I can't imagine either one.
OK. Let's see.
#106 nursed on a wire mother.
Kind of obvious, isn't it?
Gotta eat to LIVE!
But wait.

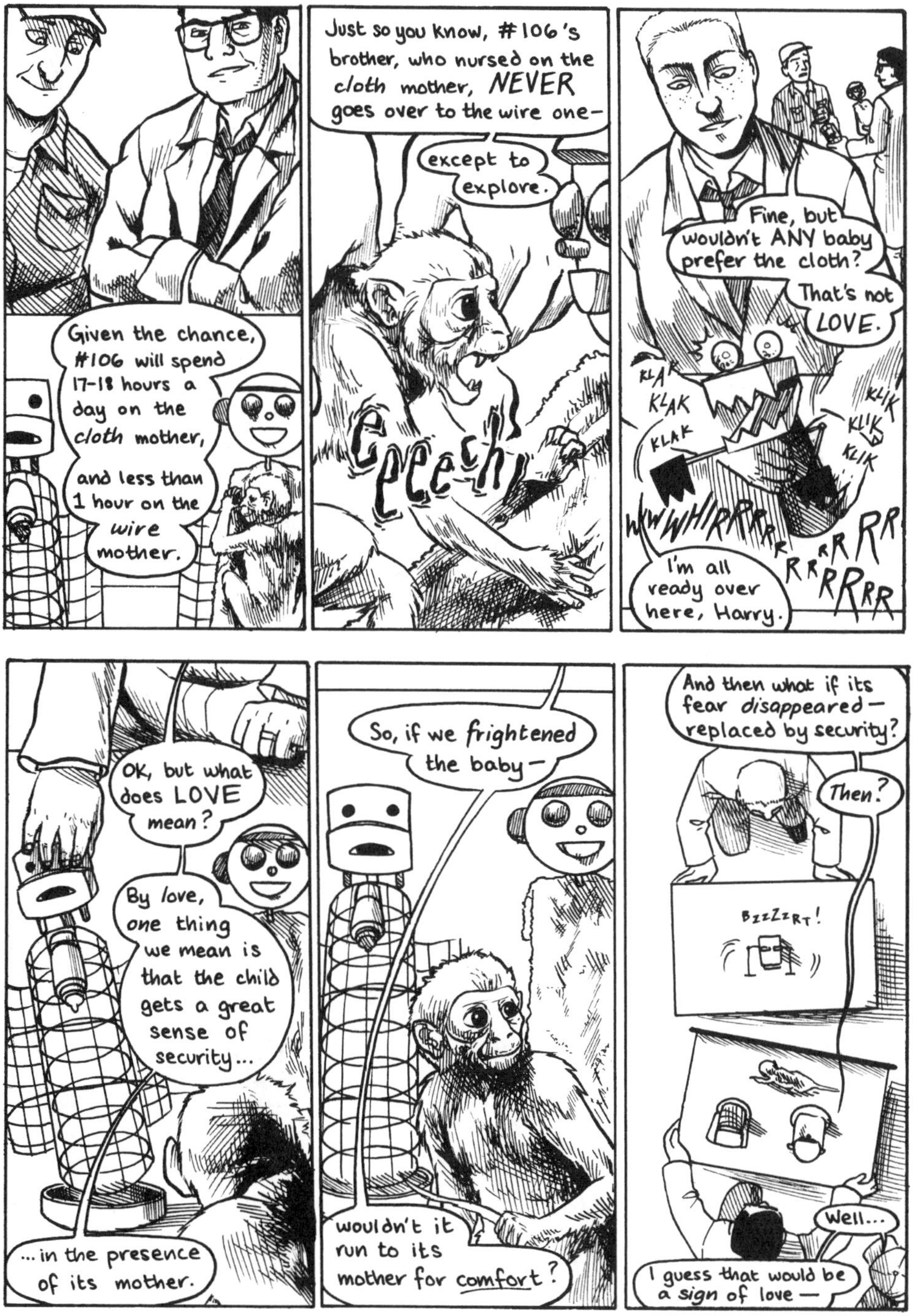
Given the chance, #106 will spend 17-18 hours a day on the cloth mother,
and less than 1 hour on the wire mother.
Just so you know, #106's brother, who nursed on the cloth mother, NEVER goes over to the wire one-
except to explore.
eeeech
Fine, but wouldn't ANY baby prefer the cloth?
That's not LOVE.
KLAK
KLAK
KLAK
KLIK
KLIK
KLIK
WWWHIRRRRRRR
RRRRRRRRR
I'm all ready over here, Harry.
OK, but what does LOVE mean?
By love, one thing we mean is that the child gets a great sense of security...
...in the presence of its mother.
So, if we frightened the baby-
wouldn't it run to its mother for comfort?
And then what if its fear disappeared- replaced by security?
Then?
BzzZzRT!
Well...
I guess that would be a sign of love-

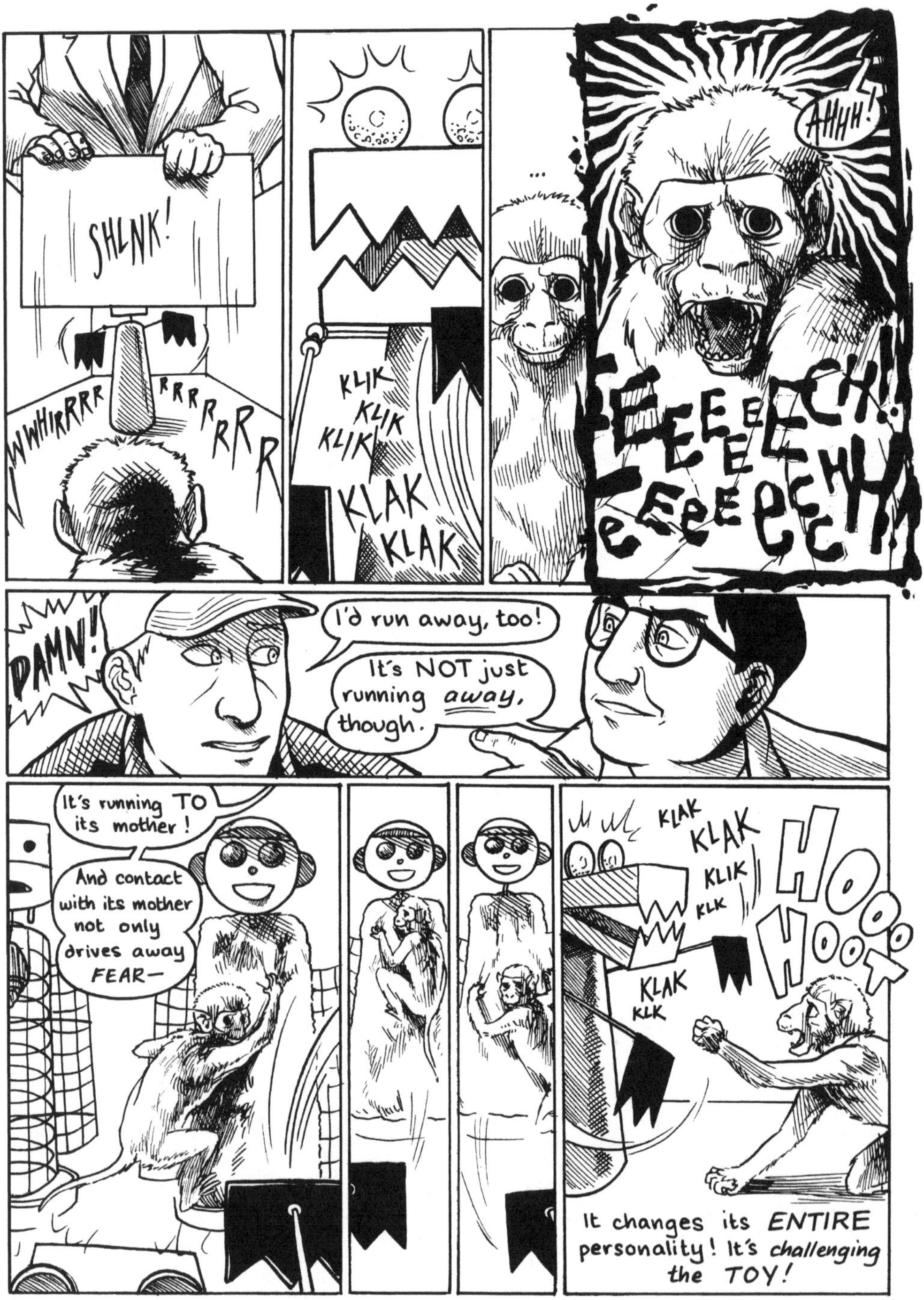
SHLNK!
WWHIRRRR RRRRRRRR
KLIK KLIK KLIK
KLAK KLAK
...
AHHH!
EEEEEECH!! EEEECHH!! eeeeech!!
DAMN!
I'd run away, too!
It's NOT just running away, though.
It's running TO its mother!
And contact with its mother not only drives away FEAR—
KLAK KLAK KLIK KLK
KLAK KLK
HOOO HOOOT
It changes its ENTIRE personality! It's challenging the TOY!

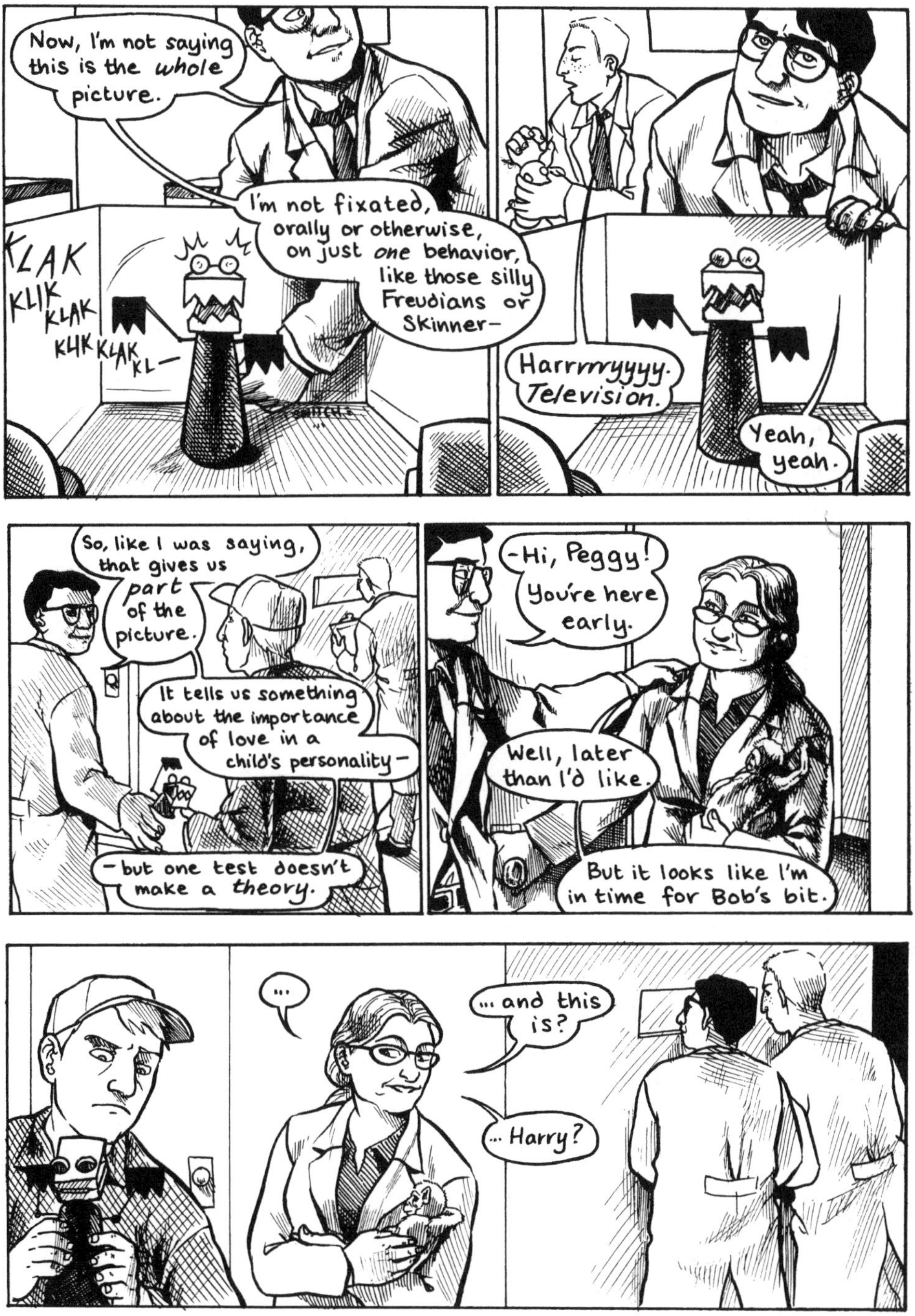
Now, I'm not saying this is the *whole* picture.
I'm not fixated, orally or otherwise, on just *one* behavior, like those silly Freudians or Skinner—
KLAK KLIK KLAK KLIK KLAK KL—
Harrrrryyyy. *Television.*
Yeah, yeah.
So, like I was saying, that gives us *part* of the picture.
It tells us something about the importance of love in a child's personality—
—but one test doesn't make a *theory*.
—Hi, Peggy! You're here early.
Well, later than I'd like.
But it looks like I'm in time for Bob's bit.
...
... and this is?
... Harry?

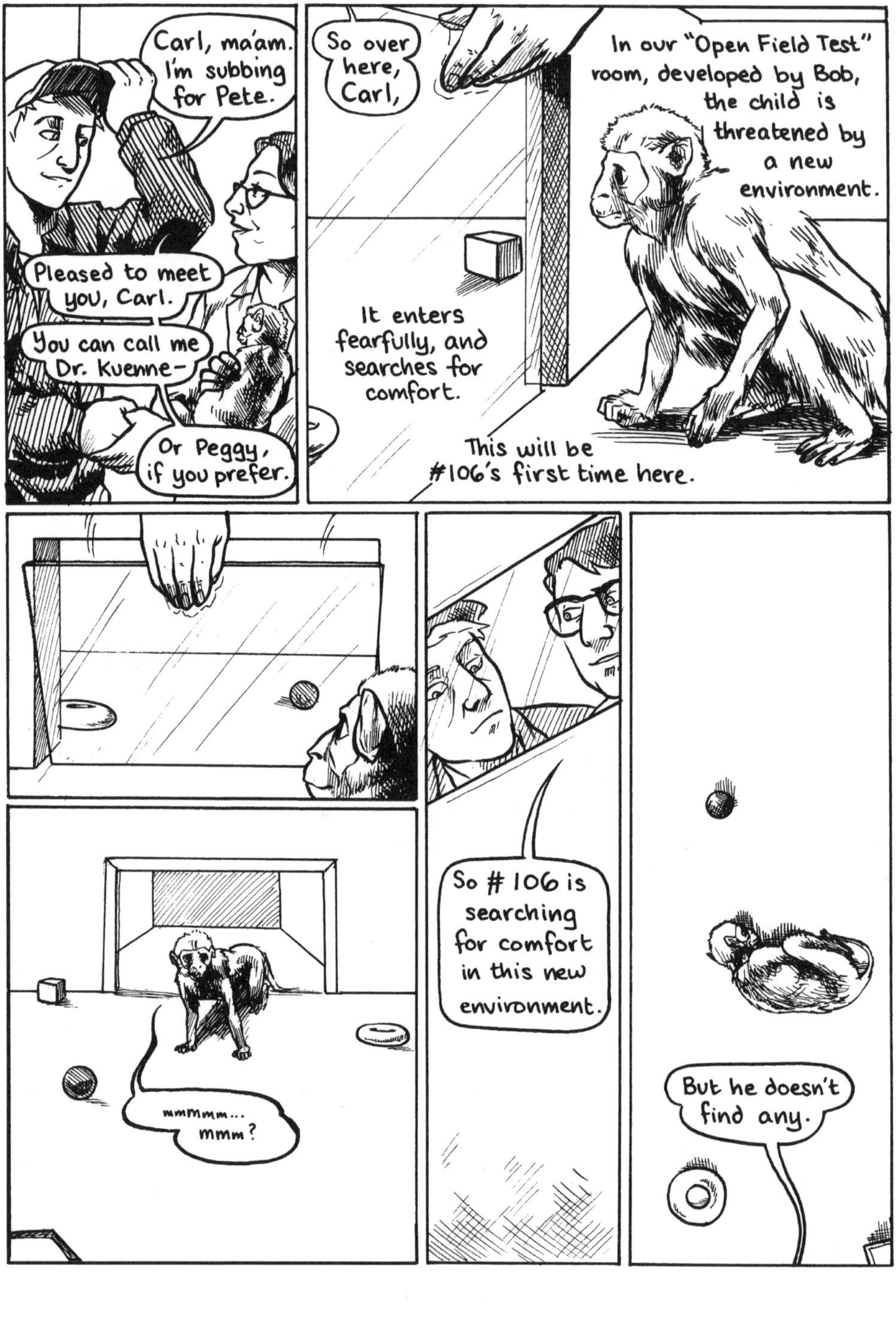
Carl, ma'am. I'm subbing for Pete.
Pleased to meet you, Carl.
You can call me Dr. Kuenne-
Or Peggy, if you prefer.
So over here, Carl,
In our "Open Field Test" room, developed by Bob, the child is threatened by a new environment.
It enters fearfully, and searches for comfort.
This will be #106's first time here.
mmmmm... mmm?
So #106 is searching for comfort in this new environment.
But he doesn't find any.

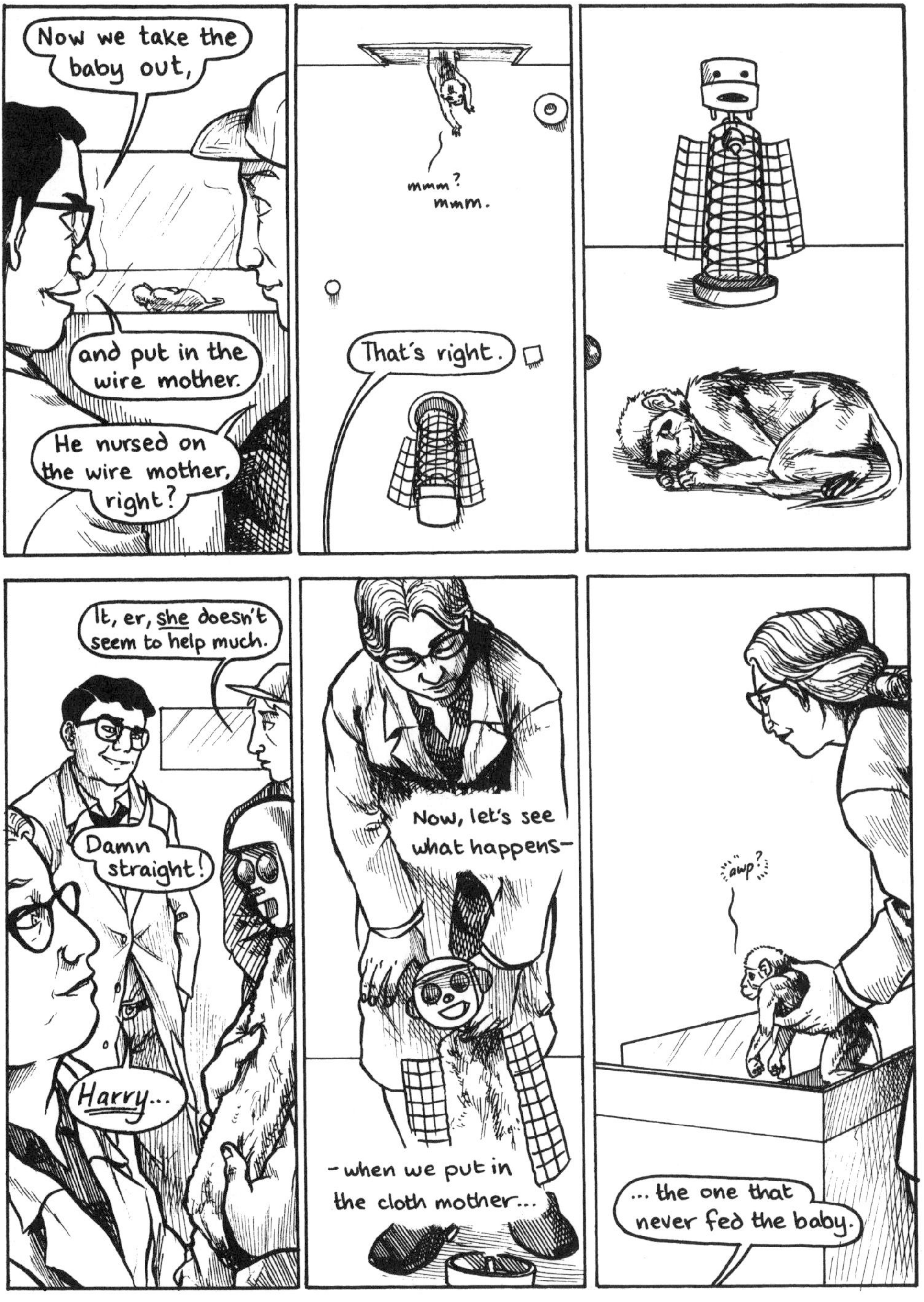
Now we take the baby out,
and put in the wire mother.
He nursed on the wire mother, right?
mmm?
mmm.
That's right.
It, er, she doesn't seem to help much.
Damn straight!
Harry...
Now, let's see what happens-
-when we put in the cloth mother...
awp?
... the one that never fed the baby.

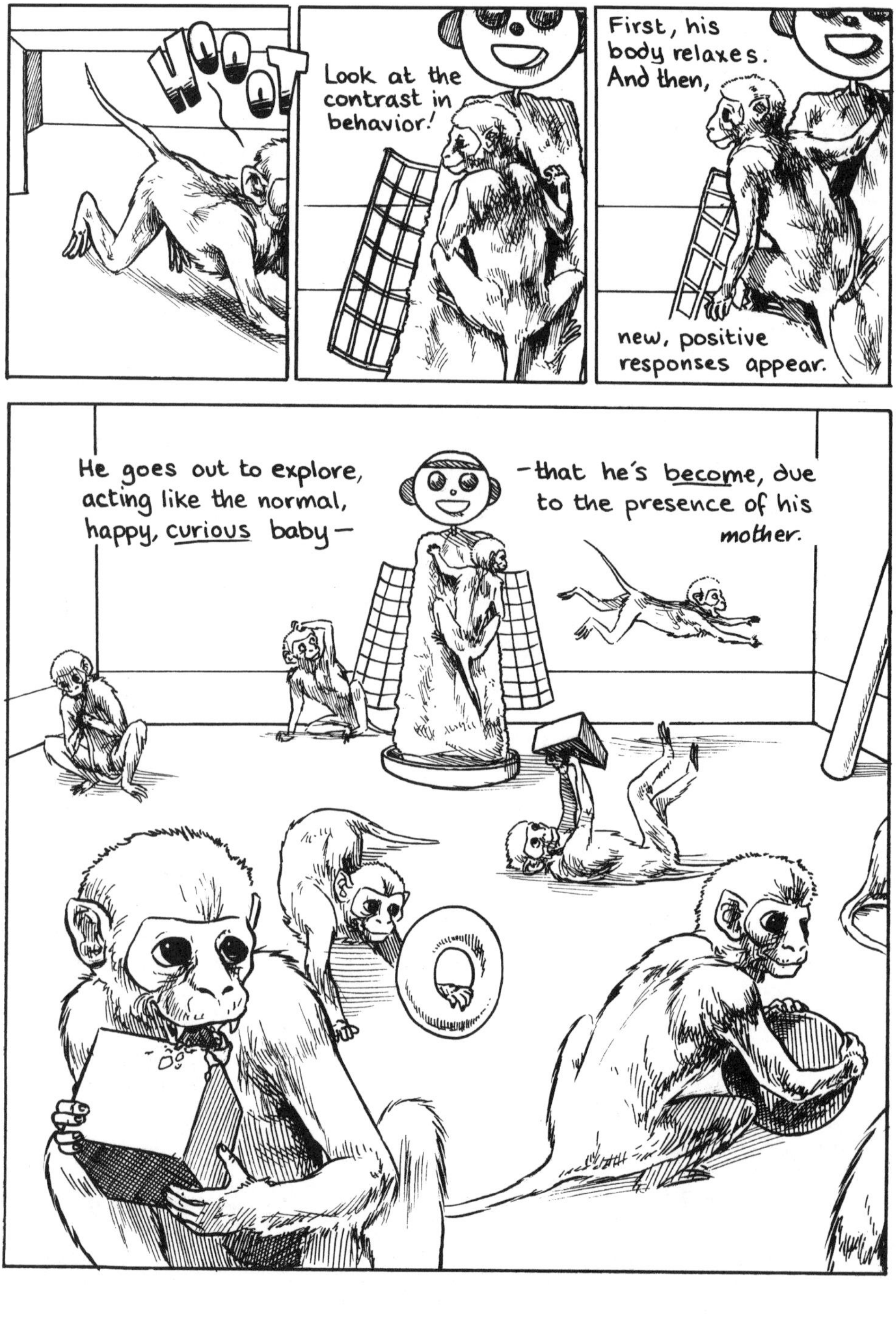
HOOOT
Look at the contrast in behavior!
First, his body relaxes. And then,
new, positive responses appear.
He goes out to explore, acting like the normal, happy, curious baby—
—that he's become, due to the presence of his mother.

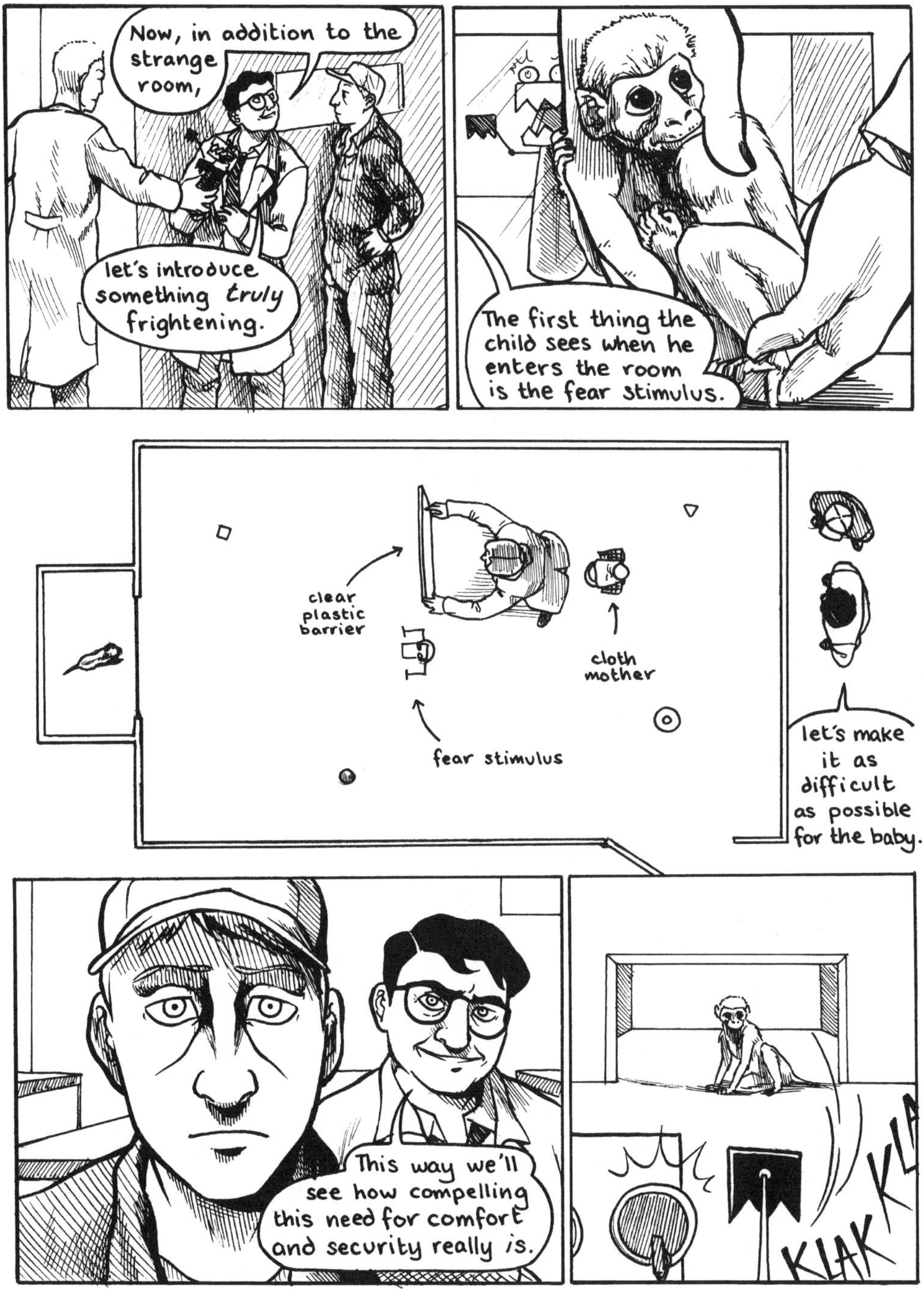
Now, in addition to the strange room,
let's introduce something *truly* frightening.
The first thing the child sees when he enters the room is the fear stimulus.
clear plastic barrier
cloth mother
fear stimulus
let's make it as difficult as possible for the baby.
This way we'll see how compelling this need for comfort and security really is.
KLAK KLA

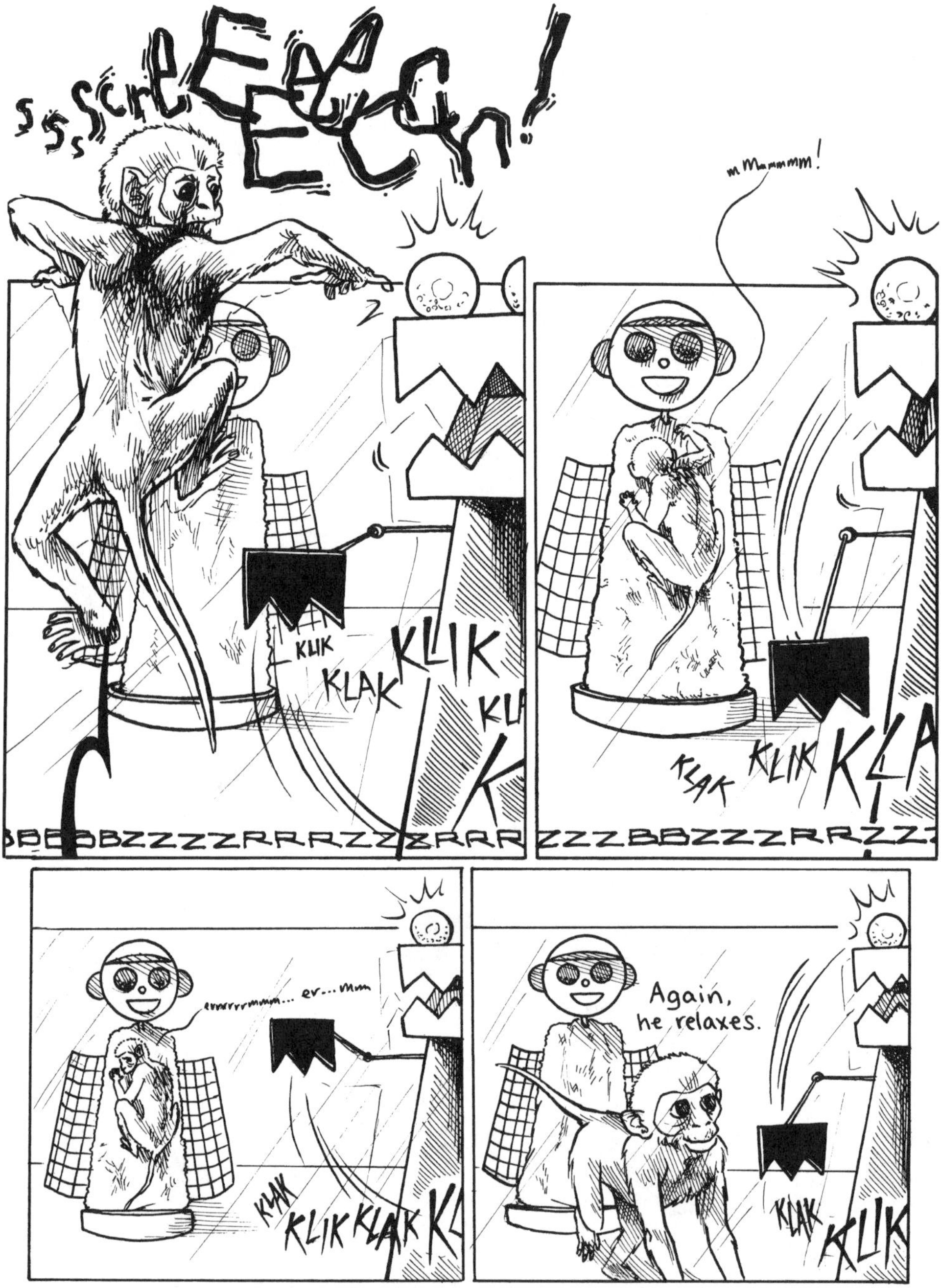
s s s scrEEeeeEEch!
KLIK
KLAK KLIK
BBBBZZZZZRRRRZZZZRRRR
mMmmmmm!
KLAK KLIK KLA
ZZZBBZZZZRRZZZ
errrrrmmm... er...mm
KLAK KLIK KLAK KL
Again, he relaxes.
KLAK KLIK

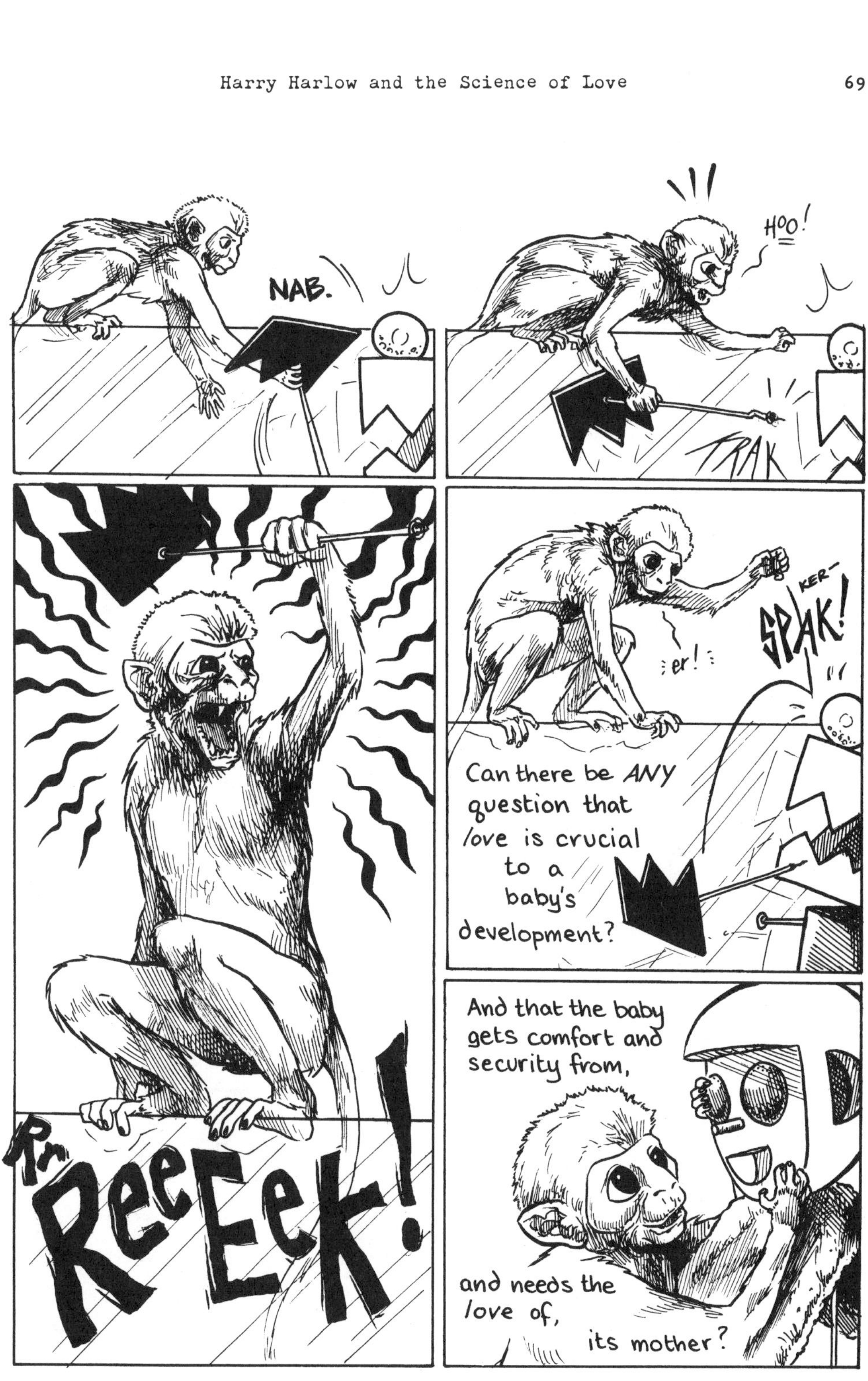
NAB.
HOO!
TRAK
RrReeEek!
er!
KER-SPAK!
Can there be ANY question that love is crucial to a baby's development?
And that the baby gets comfort and security from,
and needs the love of,
its mother?

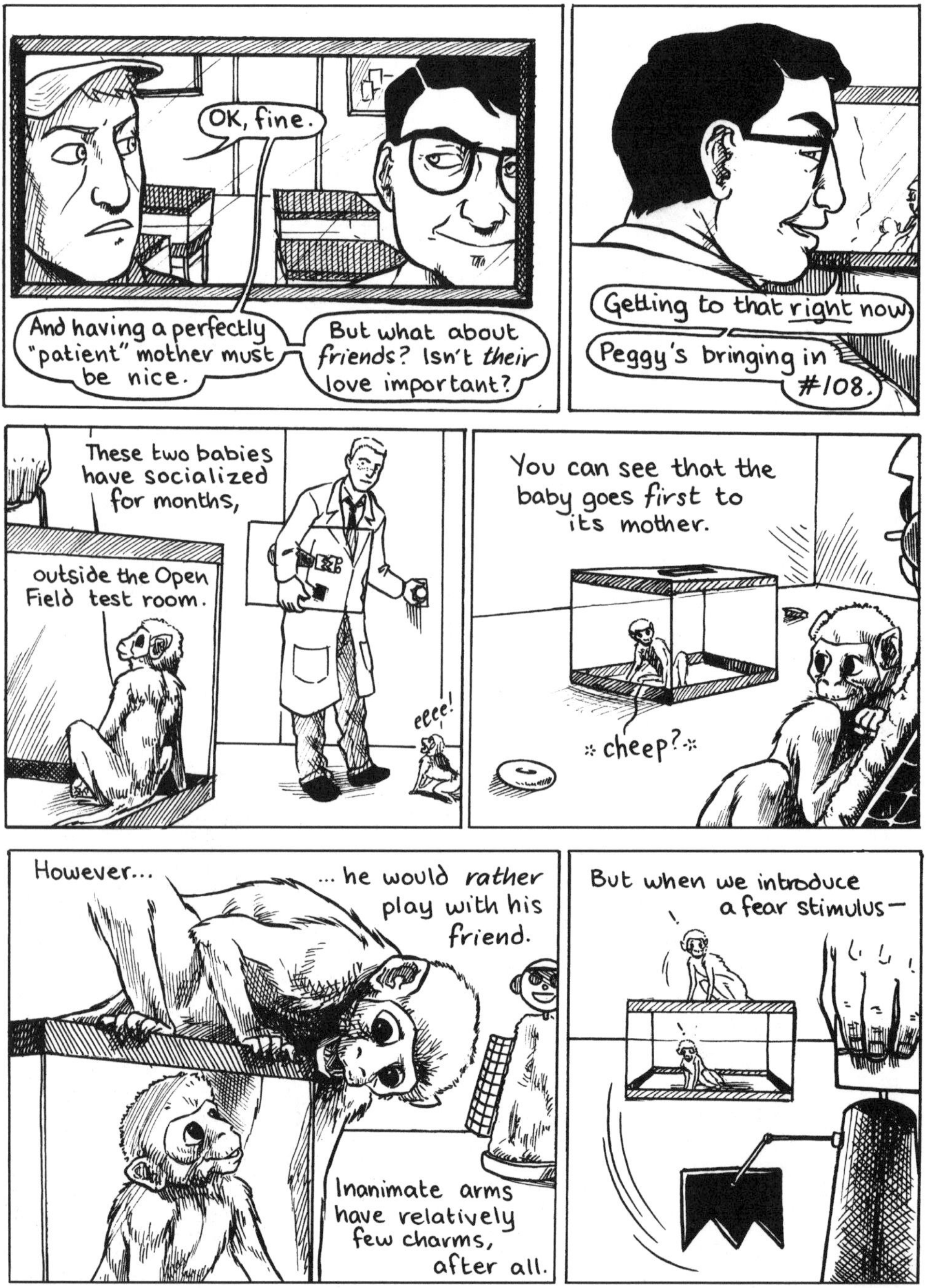
OK, fine.
And having a perfectly "patient" mother must be nice.
But what about *friends*? Isn't *their* love important?
Getting to that right now.
Peggy's bringing in #108.
These two babies have socialized for months,
outside the Open Field test room.
eeee!
You can see that the baby goes *first* to its mother.
cheep?
However...
... he would *rather* play with his friend.
Inanimate arms have relatively few charms, after all.
But when we introduce a fear stimulus—

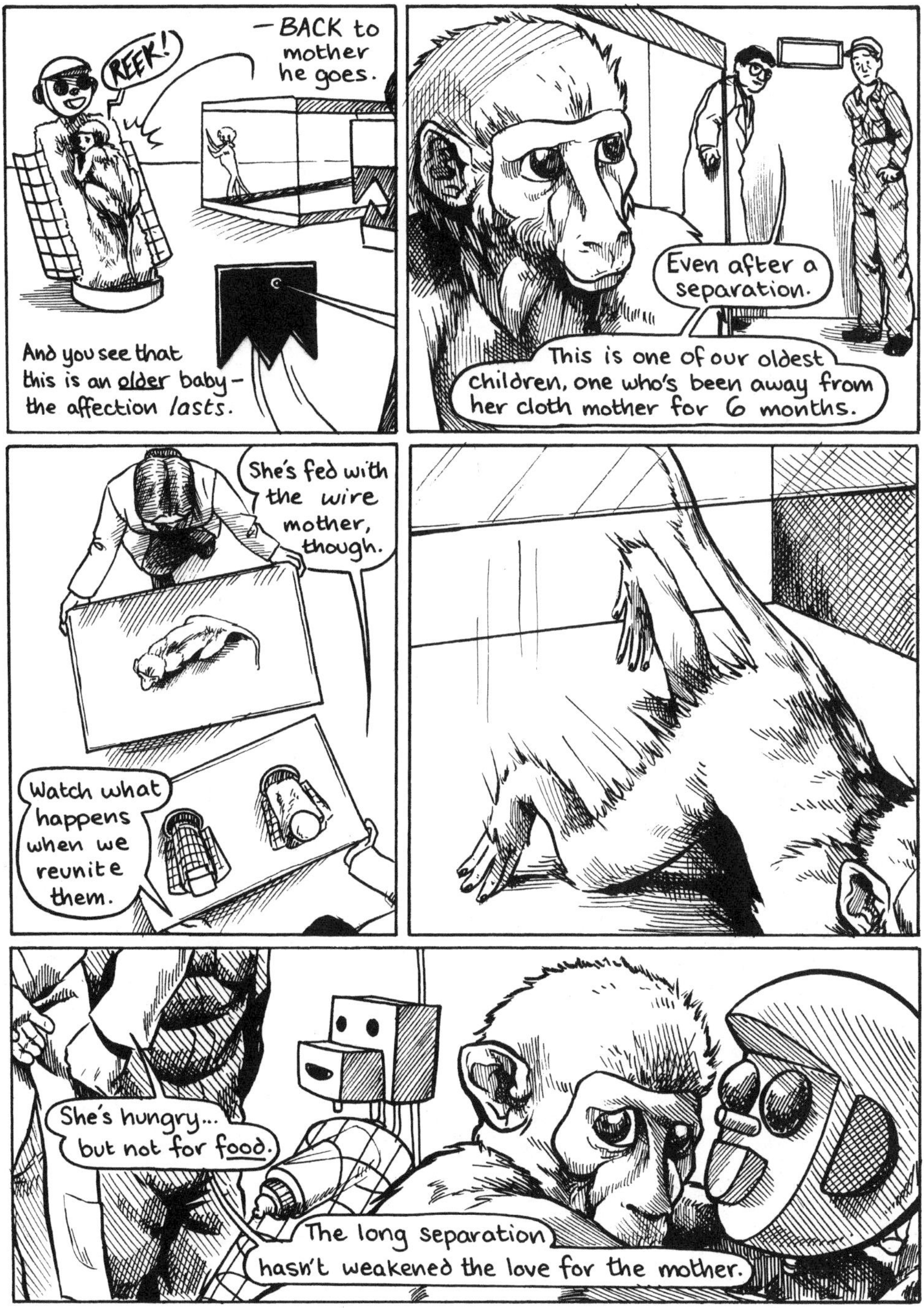
REEK!
—BACK to mother he goes.
And you see that this is an older baby— the affection lasts.
This is one of our oldest children, one who's been away from her cloth mother for 6 months.
Even after a separation.
She's fed with the wire mother, though.
Watch what happens when we reunite them.
She's hungry... but not for food.
The long separation hasn't weakened the love for the mother.

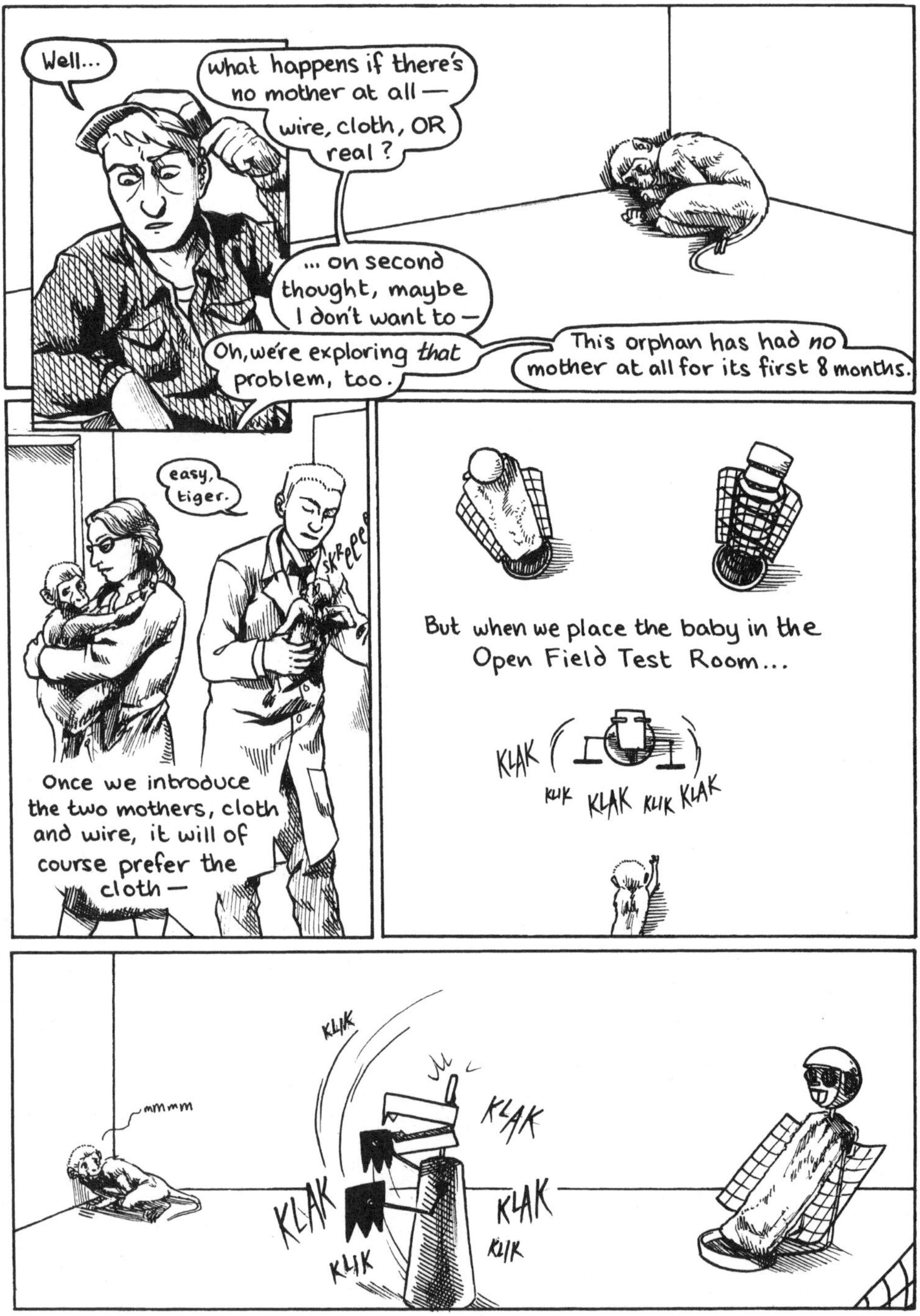
Well...
what happens if there's no mother at all — wire, cloth, OR real?
... on second thought, maybe I don't want to —
Oh, we're exploring *that* problem, too.
This orphan has had *no* mother at all for its first 8 months.
easy, tiger.
SKREEEE
Once we introduce the two mothers, cloth and wire, it will of course prefer the cloth —
But when we place the baby in the Open Field Test Room...
KLAK
KLIK KLAK KLIK KLAK
mmmm
KLIK
KLAK
KLAK
KLAK
KLIK
KLIK

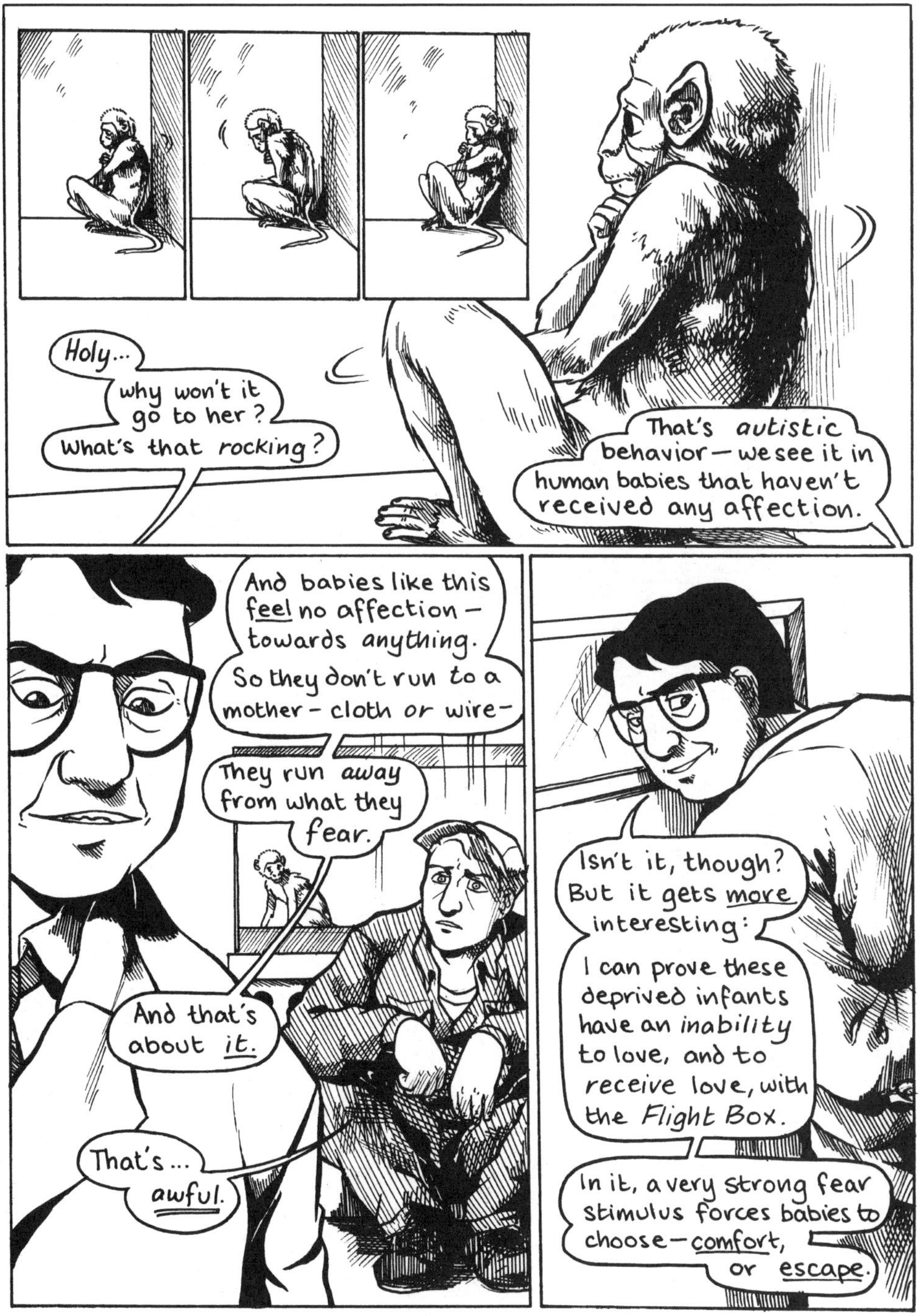
Holy...
why won't it go to her?
What's that rocking?
That's autistic behavior — we see it in human babies that haven't received any affection.
And babies like this feel no affection — towards anything.
So they don't run to a mother - cloth or wire-
They run away from what they fear.
And that's about it.
That's... awful.
Isn't it, though? But it gets more interesting:
I can prove these deprived infants have an inability to love, and to receive love, with the Flight Box.
In it, a very strong fear stimulus forces babies to choose — comfort, or escape.

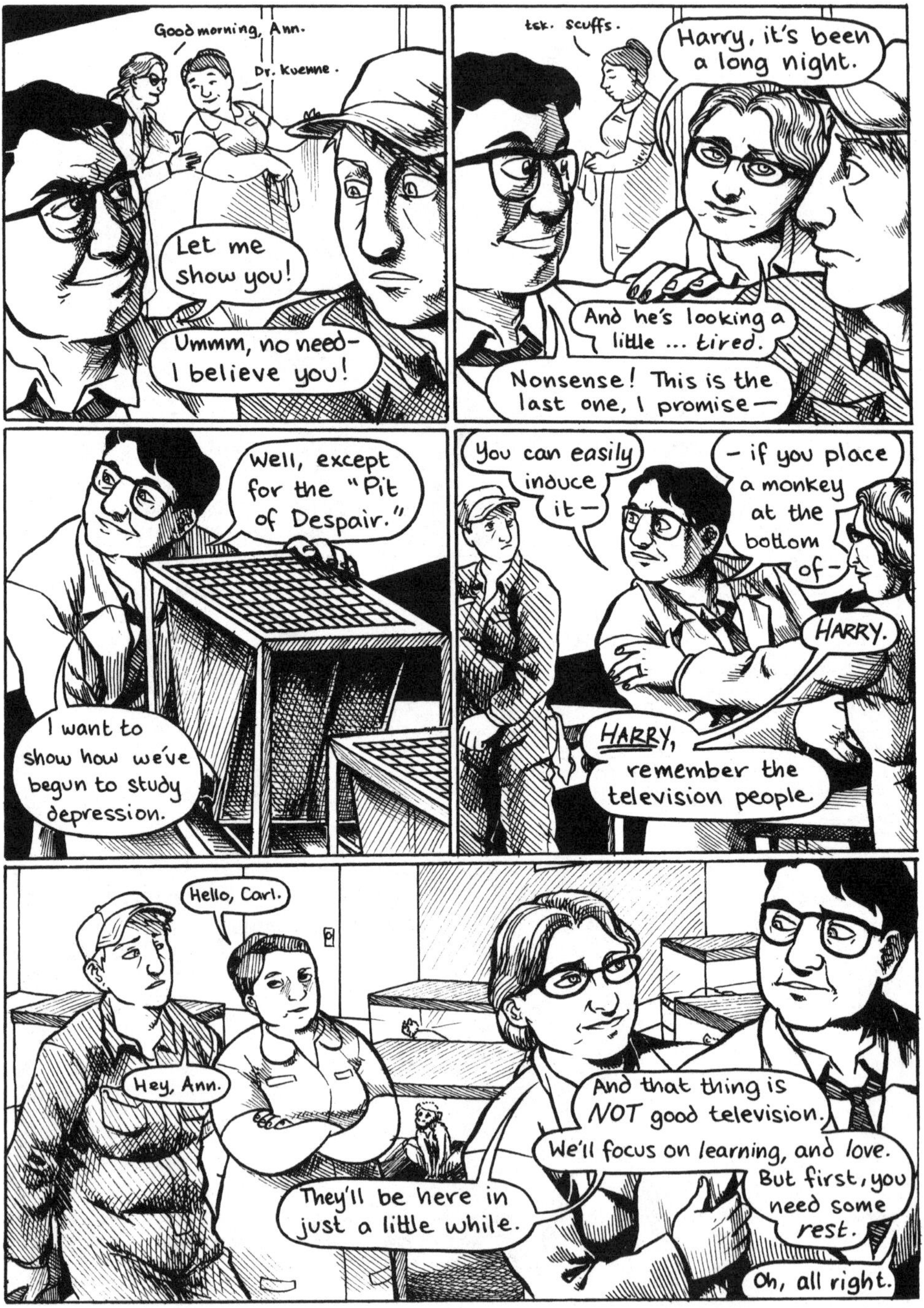
Good morning, Ann.
Dr. Kuenne.
Let me show you!
Ummm, no need- I believe you!
tsk. scuffs.
Harry, it's been a long night.
And he's looking a little ... tired.
Nonsense! This is the last one, I promise—
Well, except for the "Pit of Despair."
I want to show how we've begun to study depression.
You can easily induce it—
—if you place a monkey at the bottom of—
HARRY.
HARRY, remember the television people.
Hello, Carl.
Hey, Ann.
They'll be here in just a little while.
And that thing is NOT good television.
We'll focus on learning, and love.
But first, you need some rest.
Oh, all right.

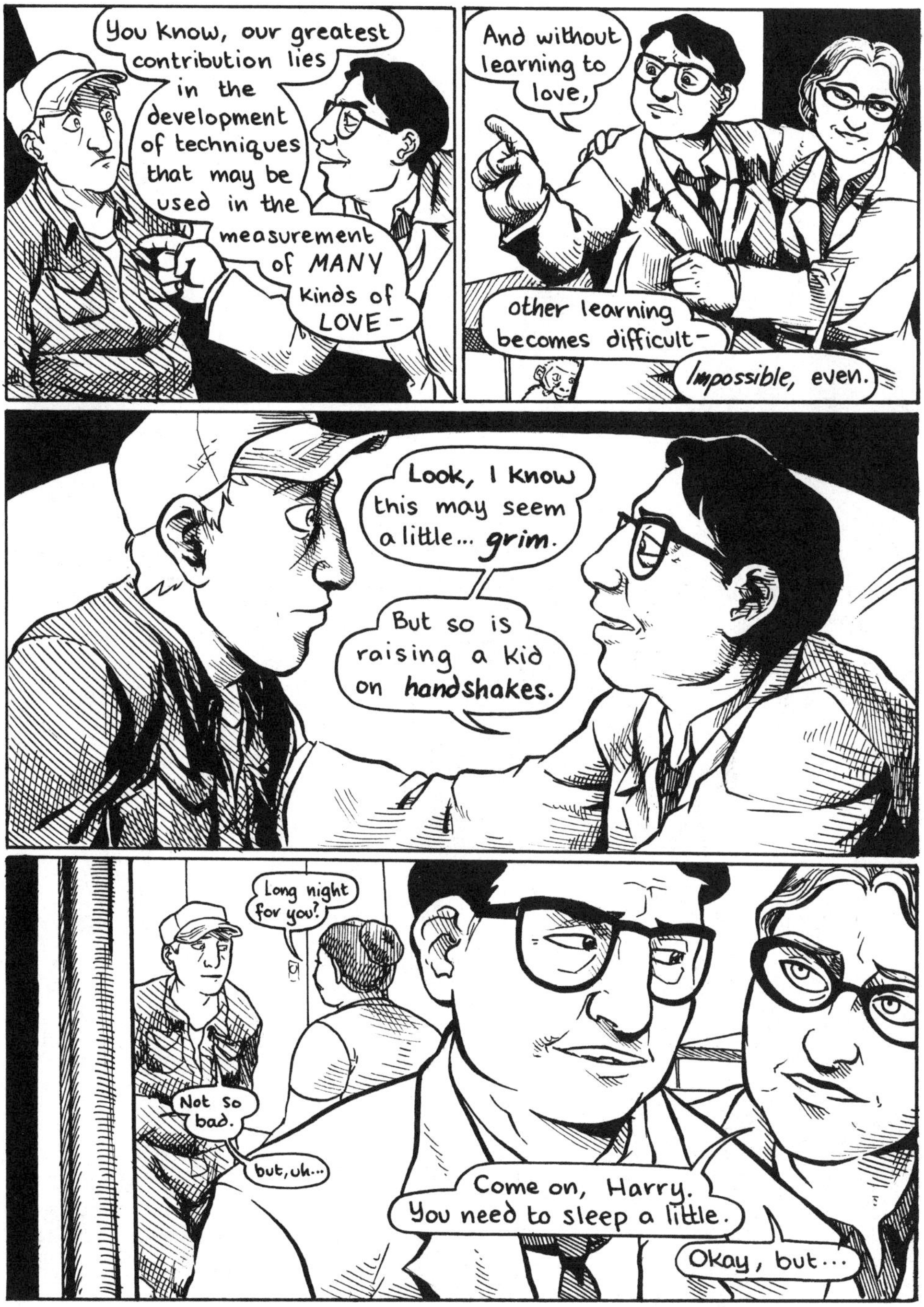
You know, our greatest contribution lies in the development of techniques that may be used in the measurement of MANY kinds of LOVE -
And without learning to love,
other learning becomes difficult -
Impossible, even.
Look, I know this may seem a little... grim.
But so is raising a kid on handshakes.
Long night for you?
Not so bad.
but, uh...
Come on, Harry. You need to sleep a little.
Okay, but...

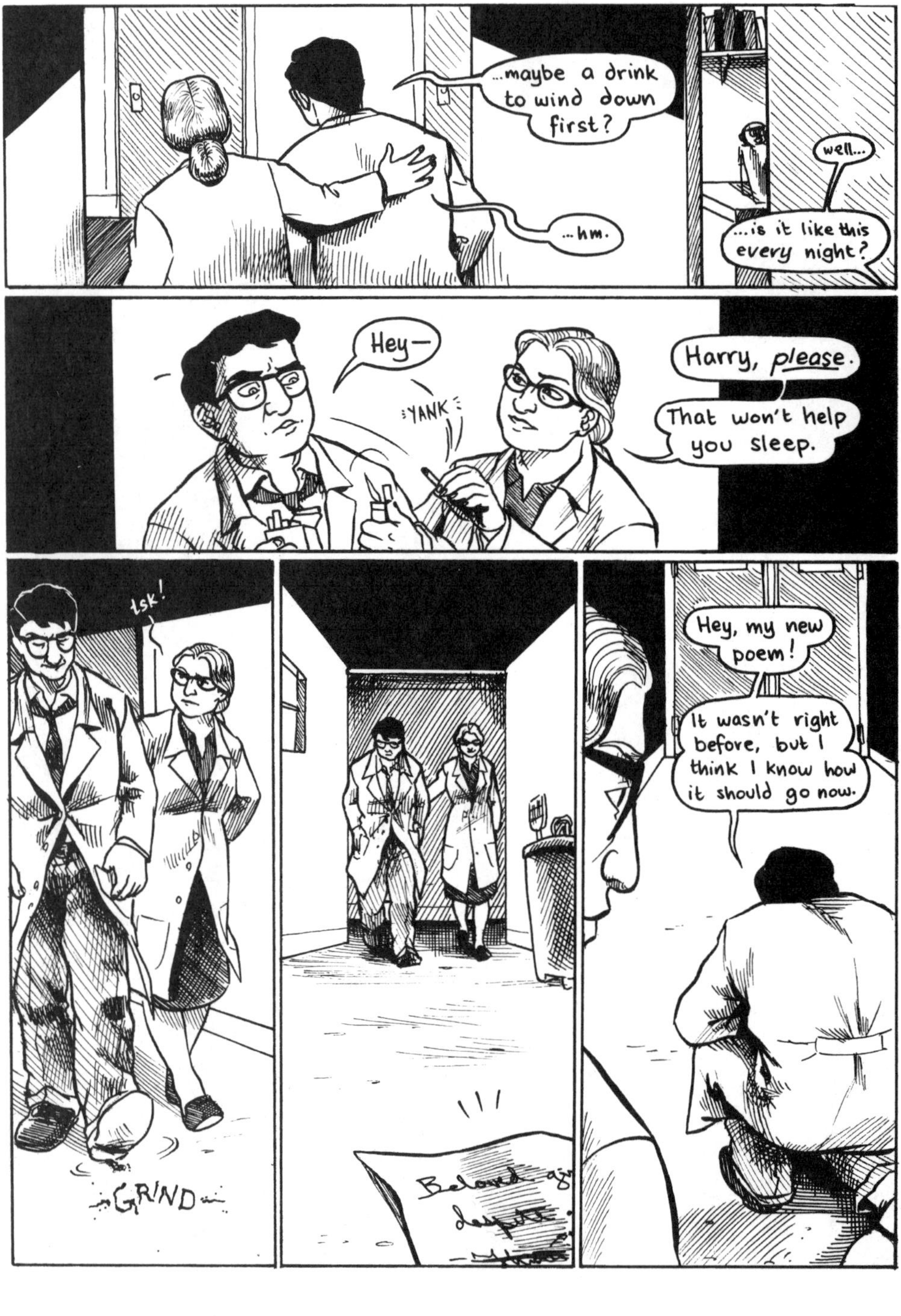
...maybe a drink to wind down first?
...hm.
well...
...is it like this every night?
Hey—
YANK
Harry, please.
That won't help you sleep.
tsk!
GRIND
Hey, my new poem!
It wasn't right before, but I think I know how it should go now.

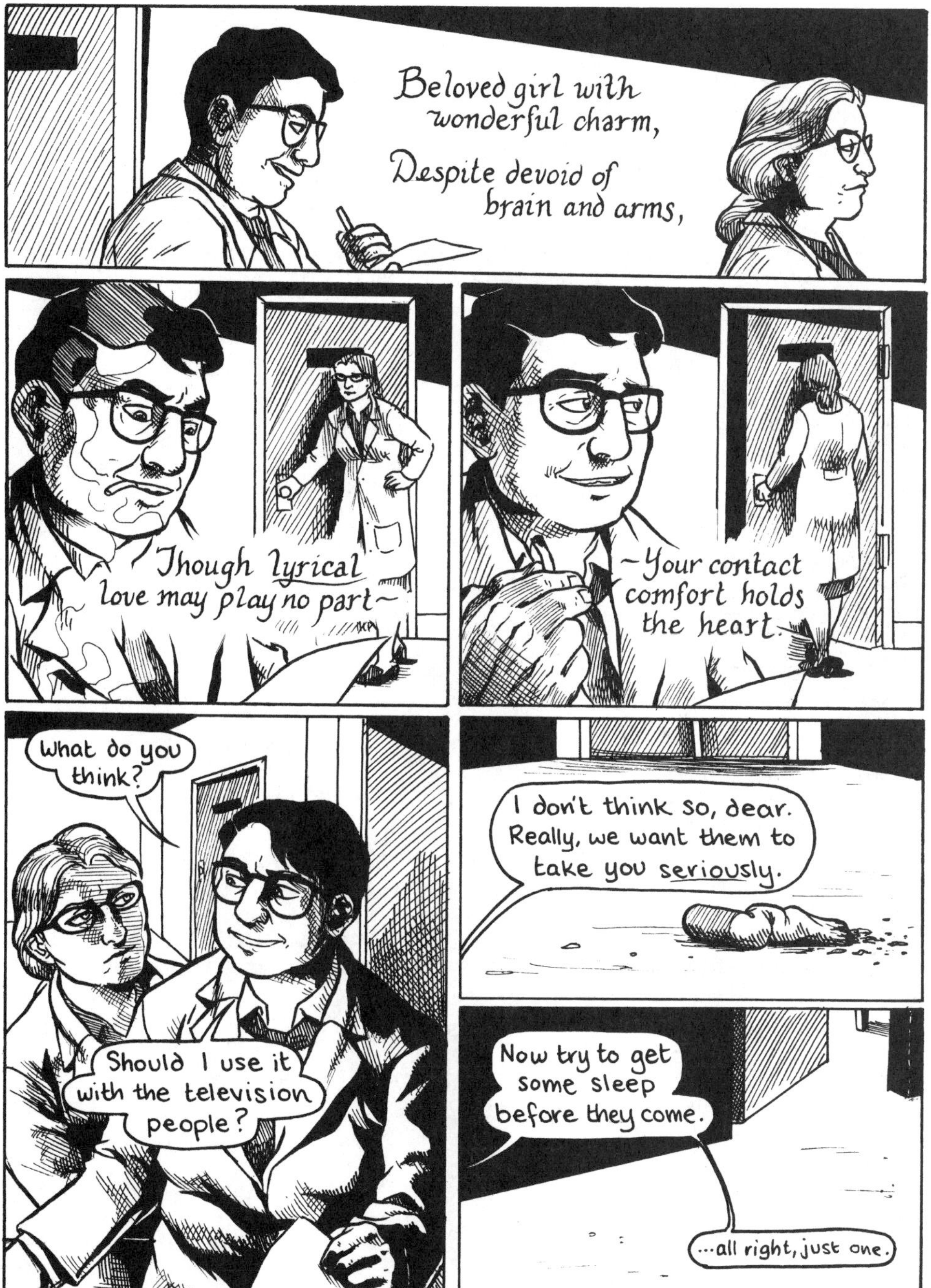
Beloved girl with wonderful charm,
Despite devoid of brain and arms,
Though lyrical love may play no part~
~Your contact comfort holds the heart.
What do you think?
Should I use it with the television people?
I don't think so, dear. Really, we want them to take you seriously.
Now try to get some sleep before they come.
...all right, just one.

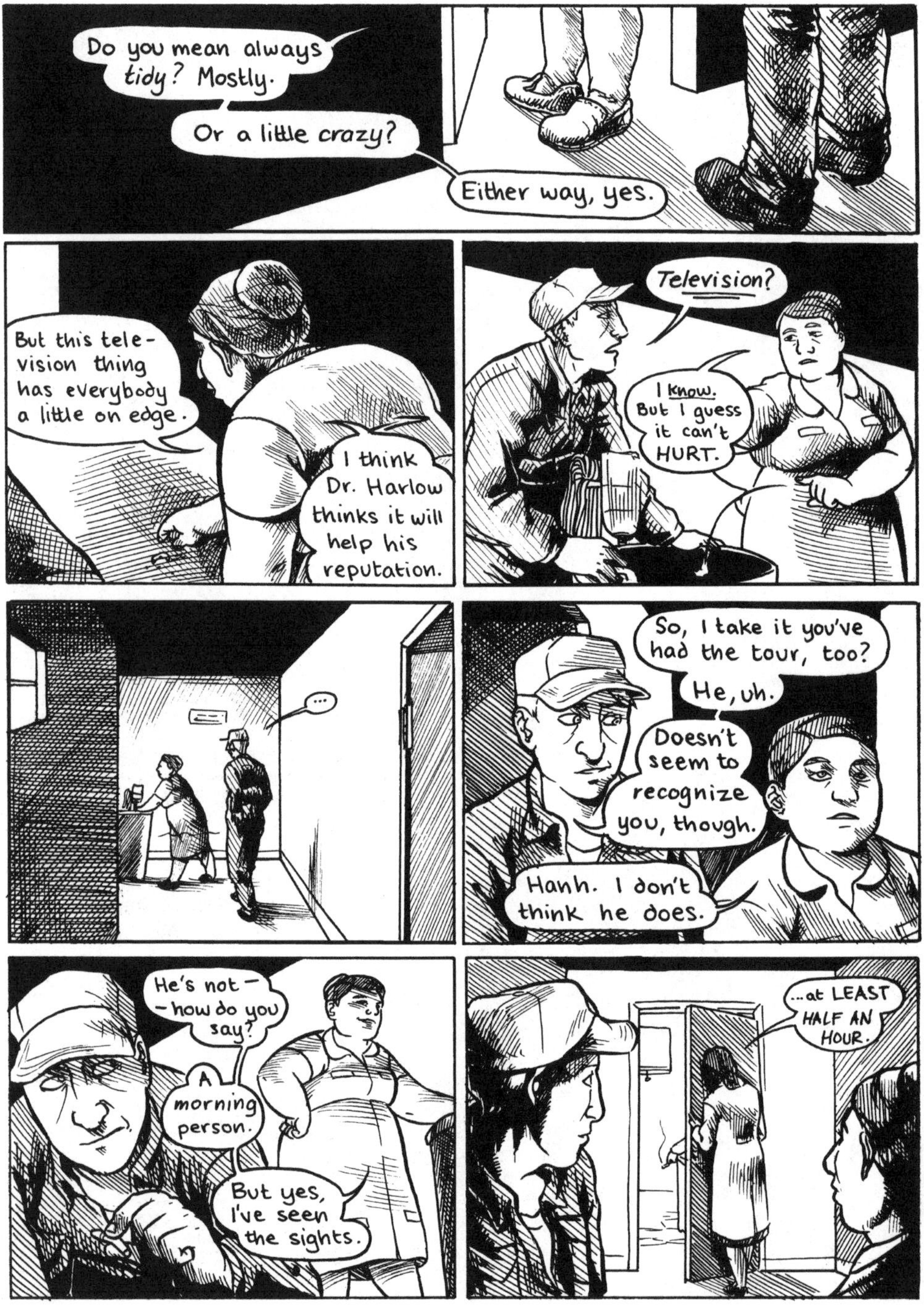
Do you mean always tidy? Mostly.
Or a little crazy?
Either way, yes.
But this television thing has everybody a little on edge.
I think Dr. Harlow thinks it will help his reputation.
Television?
I know. But I guess it can't HURT.
...
So, I take it you've had the tour, too?
He, uh.
Doesn't seem to recognize you, though.
Hanh. I don't think he does.
He's not — how do you say?
A morning person.
But yes, I've seen the sights.
...at LEAST HALF AN HOUR.

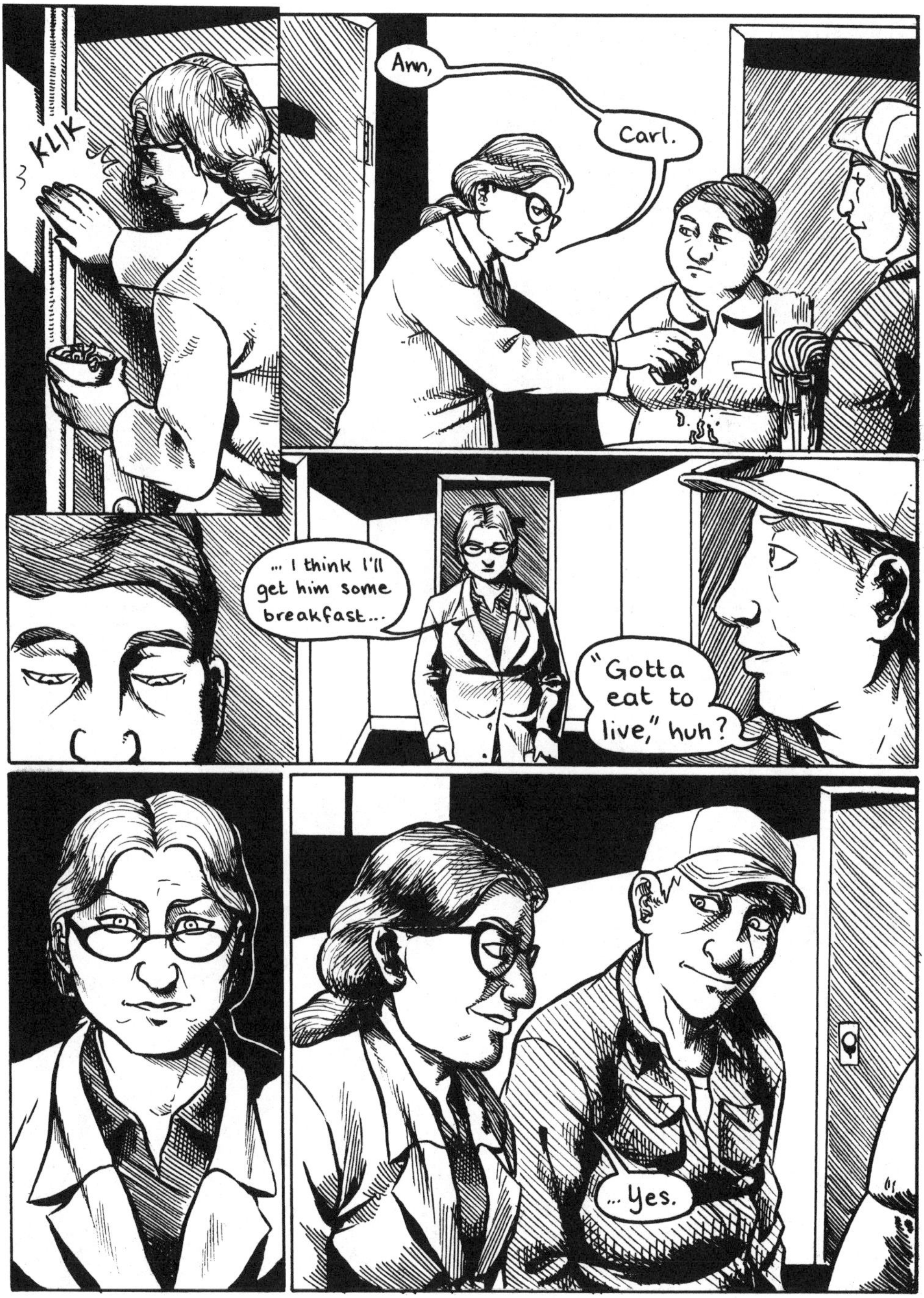
KLIK
Ann,
Carl.
... I think I'll get him some breakfast...
"Gotta eat to live," huh?
... Yes.

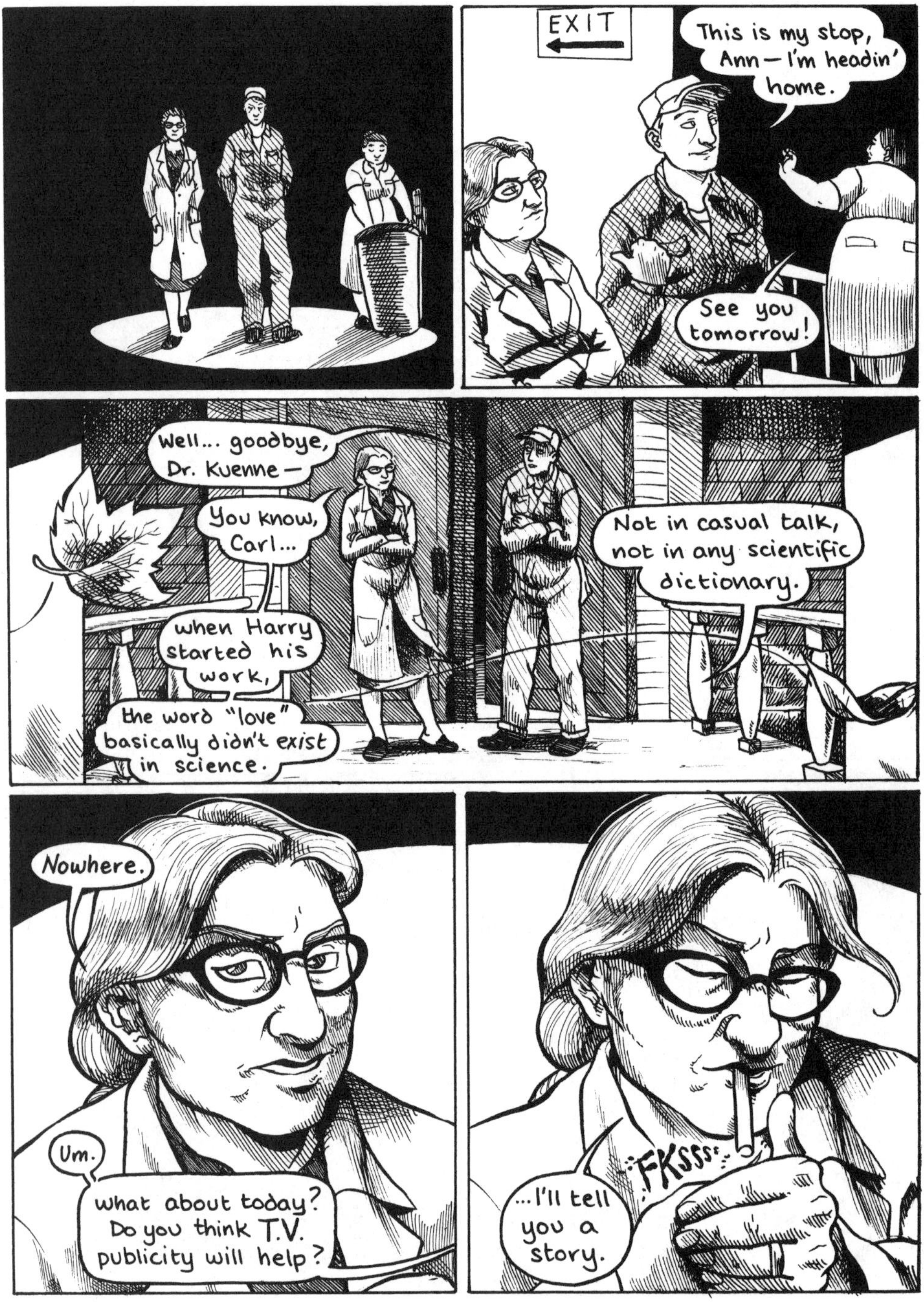
EXIT
This is my stop, Ann — I'm headin' home.
See you tomorrow!
Well... goodbye, Dr. Kuenne —
You know, Carl...
when Harry started his work,
the word "love" basically didn't exist in science.
Not in casual talk, not in any scientific dictionary.
Nowhere.
Um.
what about today? Do you think T.V. publicity will help?
FKSSS
...I'll tell you a story.

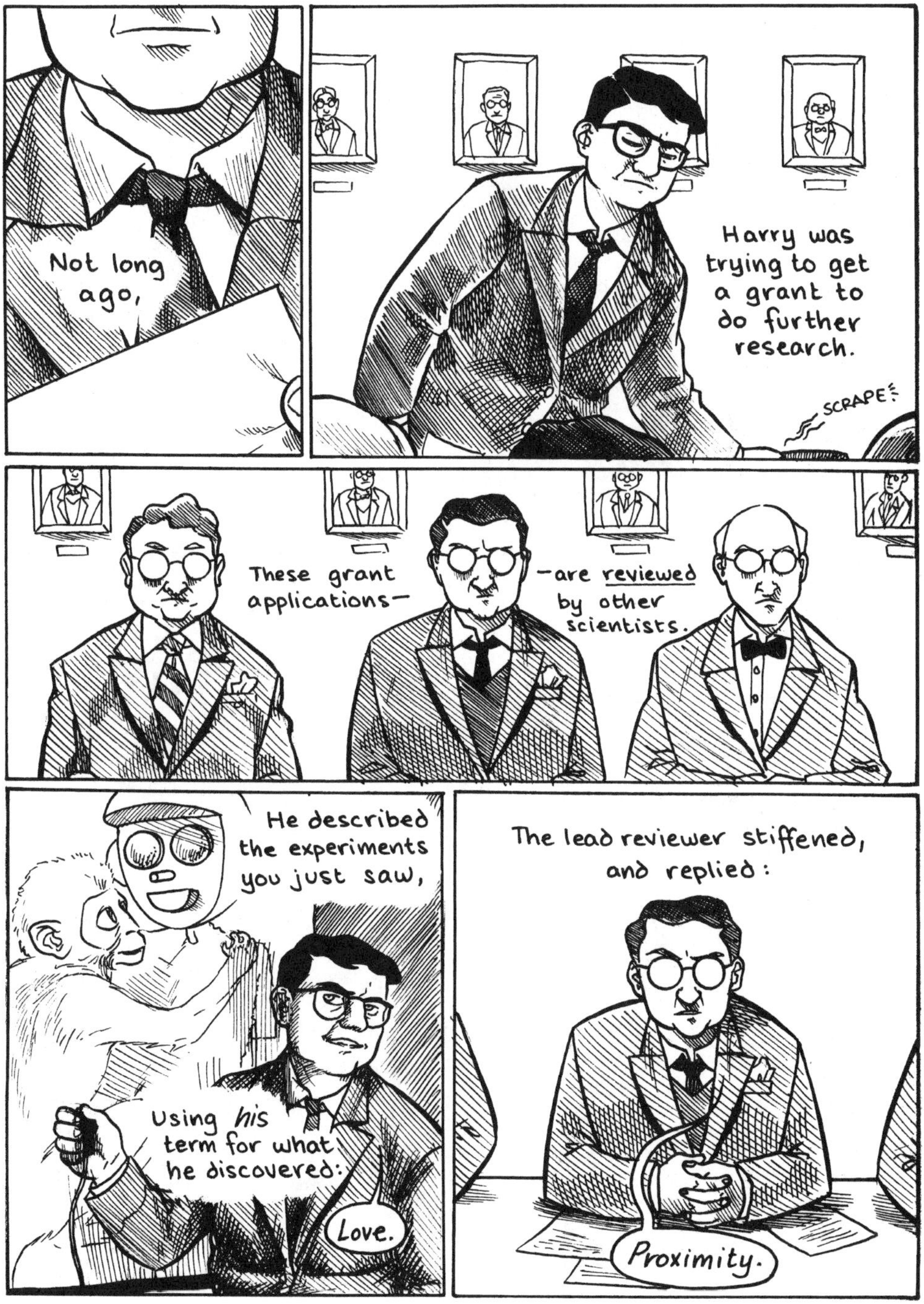
Not long ago,
Harry was trying to get a grant to do further research.
SCRAPE
These grant applications—
—are reviewed by other scientists.
He described the experiments you just saw,
Using his term for what he discovered:
Love.
The lead reviewer stiffened, and replied:
Proximity.

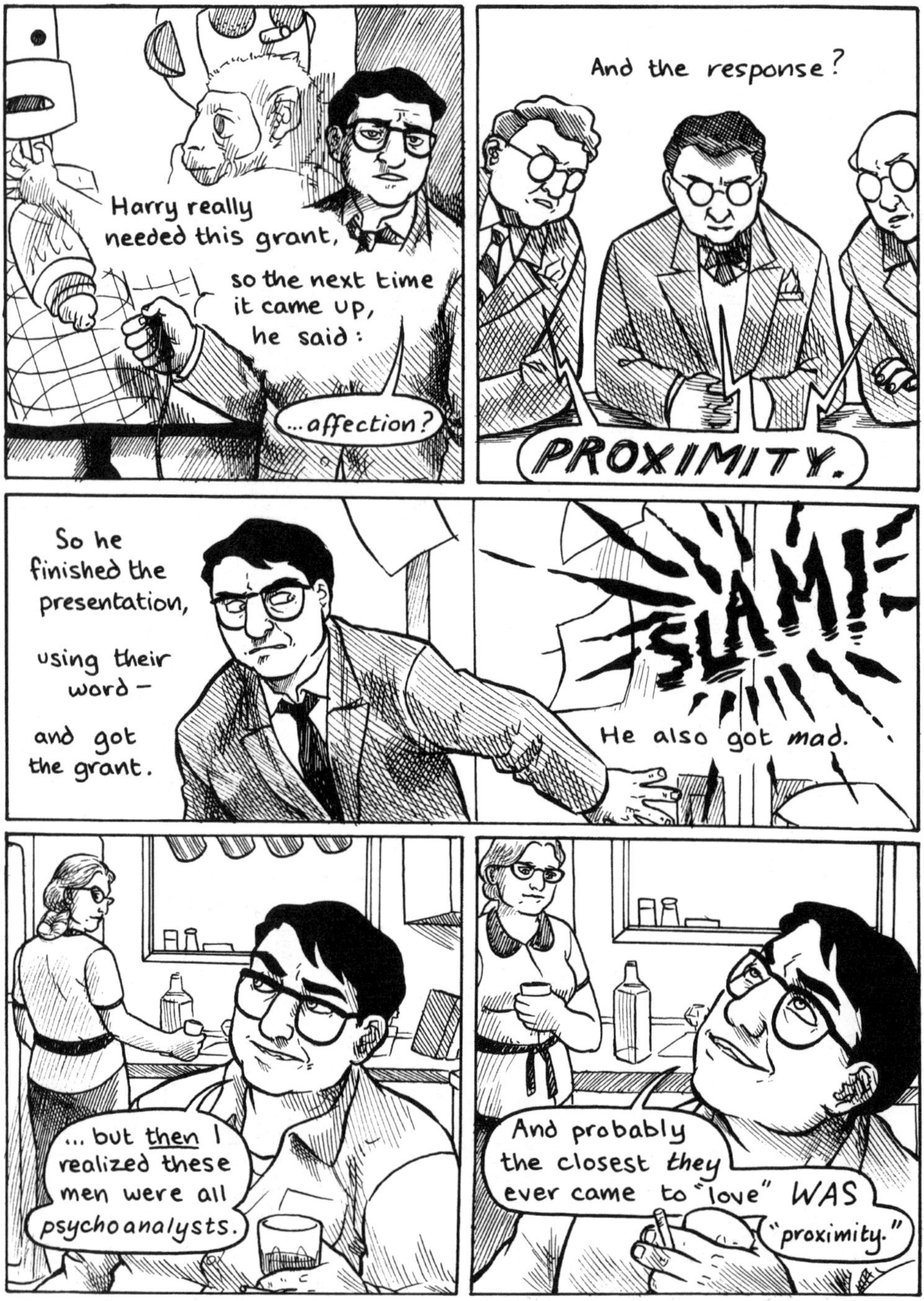
Harry really needed this grant,
so the next time it came up, he said:
...affection?
And the response?
PROXIMITY.
So he finished the presentation,
using their word –
and got the grant.
SLAM!
He also got mad.
... but then I realized these men were all psychoanalysts.
And probably the closest they ever came to "love" WAS "proximity."

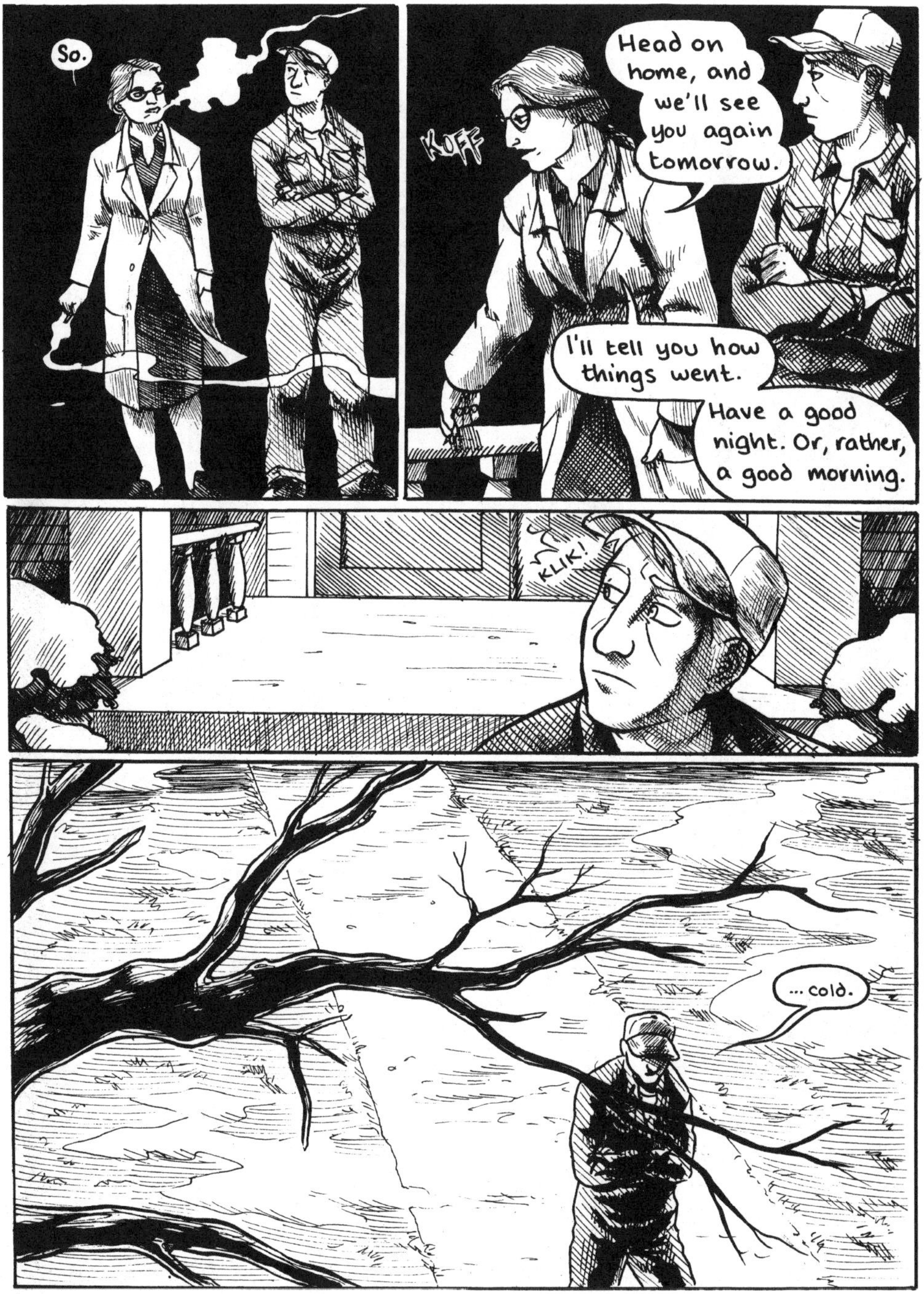
So.
KOFF
Head on home, and we'll see you again tomorrow.
I'll tell you how things went.
Have a good night. Or, rather, a good morning.
KLIK!
...cold.

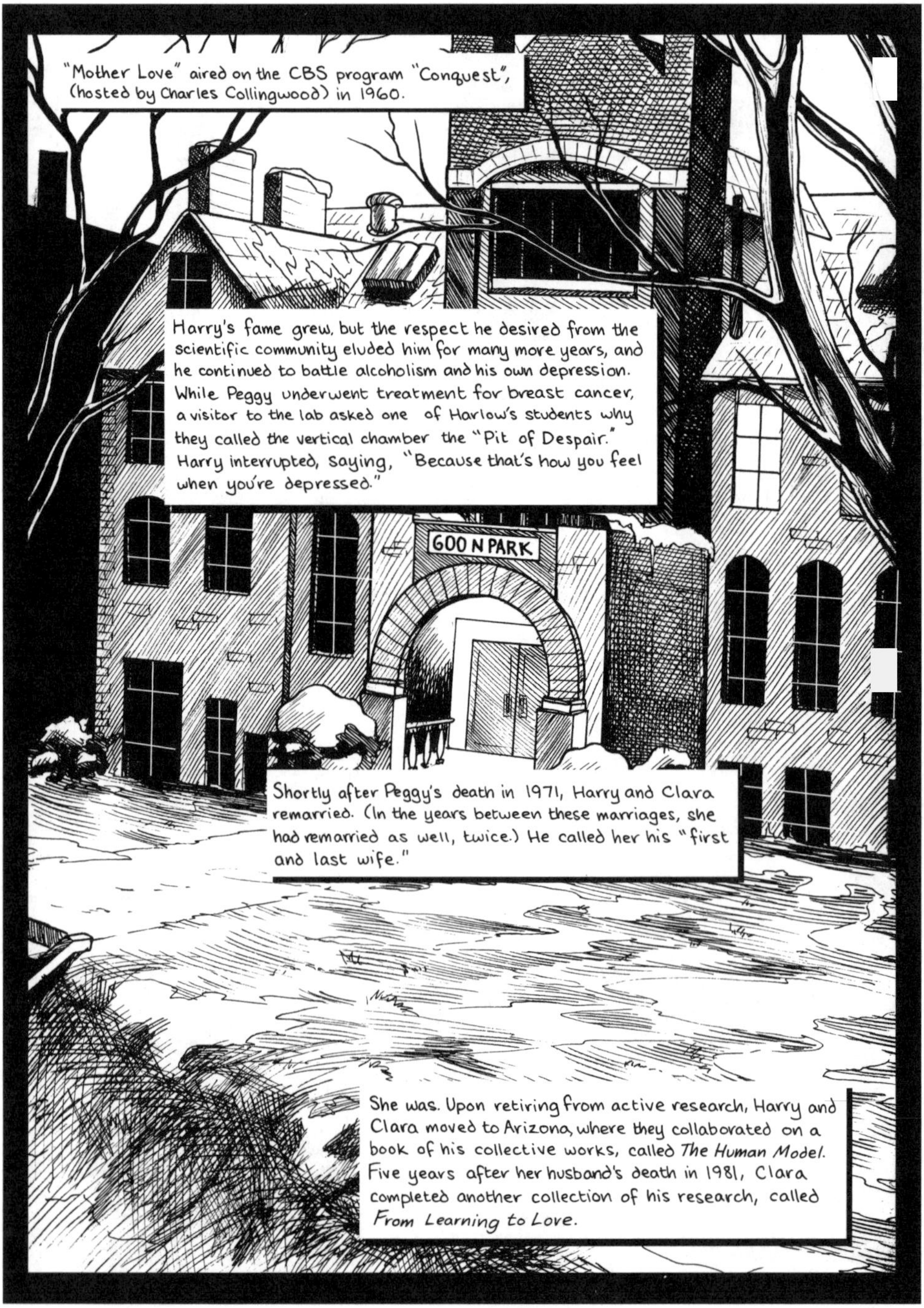
"Mother Love" aired on the CBS program "Conquest", (hosted by Charles Collingwood) in 1960.
Harry's fame grew, but the respect he desired from the scientific community eluded him for many more years, and he continued to battle alcoholism and his own depression. While Peggy underwent treatment for breast cancer, a visitor to the lab asked one of Harlow's students why they called the vertical chamber the "Pit of Despair." Harry interrupted, saying, "Because that's how you feel when you're depressed."
GOON PARK
Shortly after Peggy's death in 1971, Harry and Clara remarried. (In the years between these marriages, she had remarried as well, twice.) He called her his "first and last wife."
She was. Upon retiring from active research, Harry and Clara moved to Arizona, where they collaborated on a book of his collective works, called *The Human Model*. Five years after her husband's death in 1981, Clara completed another collection of his research, called *From Learning to Love*.

Recommended Reading

Deborah Blum, *Love at Goon Park: Harry Harlow and the Science of Affection* (Cambridge, MA: Perseus, 2002). The one book to read about Harlow's life, and his work.

Clara Mears Harlow (ed.), *From Learning to Love: The Selected Papers of H.F. Harlow* (NY: Praeger Publishers, 1986). This comprehensive overview of Harlow's scientific career, presented via his original scientific papers, is remarkable in a number of ways, but the two most important features of this book are Clara Mears Harlow's biographical sketch of her husband and how accessible the work is to a non-specialist reader.

Harry Harlow, "Autobiography," published in *Discovery Processes in Modern Biology: People and Processes in Biological Discovery*, edited by W.R. Klemm (Huntington, NY: R.E. Krieger Publishing, 1977). I used both the published version and unpublished/unedited manuscripts of this piece. Even in the published version, the editor couldn't stop Harlow from sounding like himself. Thanks to the University of Wisconsin (Madison) Department of Special Collections in the Memorial Library for providing access to this and other manuscripts.

Harry Harlow, "Monkeys, Men, Mice, Motives, and Sex," Chapter 1 of *Psychological Research: The Inside Story*, edited by Michael H. Siegel and H. Philip Zeigler (NY: Harper & Row, 1976). Here again I used published and unpublished versions, which are quite similar...the jokes and puns are tightened up and generally better in the published version!

Harry Harlow, "My Life With Men and Monkeys" (transcript of an address given at the University Club, Madison, Wisconsin, in 1959). Harlow's humor and intelligence is even more unmistakable when captured live.

Harry Harlow, "The Nature of Love," (Address of the President at the 66th Annual Convention of the American Psychological Association, Washington, D.C., August 31, 1958) first published in *American Psychologist*, vol. 13, 573-585. The paper that started it all is compelling, convincing, and readable.

Harry Harlow, "Studies with Stagner, From Laboratory to License," "The Meaning of Motherhood," and other miscellaneous unpublished documents and letters. The Harry F. Harlow papers at the University of Wisconsin (Madison) Archives in the Memorial Library provided much of the material that allowed Harlow to come to life in these pages. He was particularly cutting and witty in his personal letters, and the anecdote about love, affection, proximity, and psychoanalysts comes from a letter he wrote to Dr. Robert Perloff in 1977.

James Lileks, *Mommy Knows Worst: Highlights from the Golden Age of Bad Parenting Advice* (NY: Three Rivers Press, 2005). Much less serious than any of the other books listed here, this book has some amusing (in an "I can't believe they believed that!" sort of way) examples of bad parenting advice from bygone days. Perhaps it does have a serious subtext, though: Years from now someone will probably write a book about the ridiculous things we—and the current crop of experts—believed about parenting.

CBS Television Network, "Mother Love," from *Conquest* hosted by Charles Collingswood (NY: Carousel Film & Video, 1960, 1995). It turns out that this was very good television.

B.F. Skinner, *The Shaping of a Behaviorist: Part Two of an Autobiography* (NY: Alfred A. Knopf, 1979). Though this book reads more like a sequence of anecdotes than a story, it's still a fascinating account of Skinner, his work, and how that work intersected with his personal life.

John B. Watson, *Psychological Care of Infant and Child* (NY: W.W. Norton & Company, 1928). Remarkably, this was reprinted in 1972, so even long after Harlow's work young mothers could still get many excellent child-rearing tips along the lines of "kissing the youngster on the forehead, or the back of the hand…would be all the petting needed for a baby to learn that it is growing up in a kindly home." The excerpts I focused on in the main story were passages Harlow had personally made note of in his own papers.

CR

Author's note

Scientific integrity and progress rely on challenging pre-conceived notions and seeking truth. Further, science has to constantly challenge *its own* findings by repeating experiments and verifying results. What one scientist does must be do-able by another.

But…

Nobody today argues that we should repeat Harry Harlow's experiments. The baby monkeys, even those raised with contact comfort, suffered permanent harm from their upbringing. Inanimate arms were and are never enough, so it's bad enough that anyone needed to do those experiments in the first place. But someone did, and thanks to Harlow and his colleagues, we know that love is as real as mathematics. It exists, it's learned, and it matters. That's all we need to know.